Making It

From Wanting a Career as a Musician to Having One

By Matthew Crumpton, Esq. & Tristan Kinsley

www.makingitbook.com

Editor: Leon Bass, Esq.

Asst. Editors: Ben Albaugh, Zackary Cramp, & Maria Schied

Cover Art by Cole Carnevale

Copyright © 2011

Dying Art Publishing™

First Edition, May 2011

Published by Dying Art Publishing

International Standard Book Number (ISBN): 978-0-578-08318-6

All rights reserved. Printed in the United States of America. This book may not be reproduced in whole or in part by mechanical means, photocopying, scanning, or any other means without written permission.

TABLE OF CONTENTS

INTRODUCTION

"You've got to hear this guy that I know," my mother said confidently. "He has a great voice, plays five instruments very well, writes amazing songs, and he has the look. He is definitely going to be on the radio one day!"

I rolled my eyes.

"I'm sure he is great, but I guarantee we will not hear him on the radio, ever," I replied to my mom with as much certainty in my voice as if I was saying 'The sky is blue.'

And then my mom said something to me that prompted the idea for this book: Why not? Someone has to do it. How do they do it?

I have heard and seen hundreds of talented artists and bands, many of whom I thought were good enough to "make it." Most of those people are now working nine-to-five jobs and do not play music for a living.

I never thought about the pursuit of a career in music with the optimism and, to an extent, naivety of my mother, who has no experience in the music industry. Turns out, it was just the push that I needed to start a year-long journey of asking questions about the state of the music industry, the rise to success, and, ultimately, relationships between artists and fans.

Why not? I guess someone does have to do it. There has to be a way to figure out how the people who are “making it” have reached their current station in life and what approach they used to get there.

With that renewed excitement about the business of music, I contacted my friend Tristan Kinsley, a Nashville entrepreneur and former member of the Americana band, The Princes of Hollywood. Together, we interviewed artists who have had successful careers and asked them a series of simple questions, with the primary inquiry being: How did you go from *wanting* a career as a musician to *having* one?

We then compiled and synthesized those interviews, looking at what each artist had in common in their respective paths to success, to put forth our thesis of what it takes to make it as an artist under the new paradigm of the music industry.

* * *

As a quick aside, it is important to discuss how we define whether an artist has had a “successful” career and has thus “made it.” There are many different opinions about success. Some believe that success requires a Top 40 radio hit. Some say it is a placement on a popular television show. Of course, those things don’t hurt.

In our eyes, however, an artist is a success story if his or her primary means of income consists of writing, recording, and/or performing music. The total annual income earned by artists interviewed in this book varies considerably. But all of the artists are living the dream of being full time professional musicians.

* * *

Our goal was to ask all of the outstanding artists whom we interviewed the same questions and find out what answers they had in common, as well as where their paths to success diverged.

After the interviews were completed, we synthesized all of the information into different topical chapters. That way, it is easy to tell what the artists thought about each issue. Then, we looked at all of the information, and all of the various paths to success, and distilled it into one very ambitious chapter (How To Make It).

We encourage you to read the entire book instead of skipping straight to the end. The other chapters provide depth and very interesting background stories.

* * *

We wrote this book because we believe that no one has ever thoroughly answered the question: How do you do it? How do you really make a career for yourself as a musician?

Artist biographies usually read something like this:

> She wrote songs, put them on MySpace, began making a name for herself across the country, and now she headlines arenas.

There are a lot of steps missing there. We want to fill in that information with the naked truth and sometimes stranger-than-fiction stories of how it was really done.

We hope that the patterns that we found to the careers of the artists we interviewed will allow up and coming artists to make smart choices about their music careers.

INTERVIEWEES

Dave Barnes

Dave Barnes is a singer/songwriter who has received praise from a number of notable artists, including John Mayer, Billy Currington, Amy Grant, and Vince Gill. In addition to his music career, Barnes is a stand-up comedian, performing the occasional sold-out comedy show. The Nashville based artist is currently signed to Razor & Tie Records. His song, *God Gave Me You*, recently topped one hundred thousand digital downloads.

www.davebarnes.com

Gabe Dixon

A truly gifted piano whiz, Gabe Dixon is a singer/songwriter who is known for his work with the Gabe Dixon Band. Dixon has played keyboards with Paul McCartney, O.A.R., Loggins & Messina, and Justin Nozuka. Dixon has had numerous song placements in film and television, most recently in *The Proposal*. He is currently signed to Fantasy Records.

www.gabedixon.com

Five Times August

Five Times August is the name for the high-achieving D.I.Y. solo project of Brad Skistimas. Five Times August was the first act not signed to a major record label to have nationwide distribution in Wal-Mart. He has appeared on CBS' *The Early Show* and has had more than fifty TV placements.

www.fivetimesaugust.com

Guster

Guster is an alternative rock band, best known for its dual vocalists, humor, and live performances. The band has released six studio records and a live DVD (Guster on Ice). It has had radio success with singles *Amsterdam*, *One Man Wrecking Machine, Satellite*, and *Do You Love Me?* The band is active in environmental issues and is constantly touring.

www.guster.com

Griffin House

Griffin House has attracted his fan base by constant touring and excellent songwriting. The Nashville based artist and accomplished golfer (he turned down a college golf scholarship), has had substantial success with film and television placements, including *One Tree Hill*, *Numbers*, *Rescue Me, Everwood*, and a number of national television commercials.

www.griffinhousemusic.com

Johnny Lee

Johnny Lee is one of the first ever country to pop crossover stars. His well-known song, *Lookin' For Love*, was simultaneously number one on the Billboard Country Charts and number two on the Billboard Pop Charts. He continues to write and record today.

www.johnnyleefanclub.com

Erin McCarley

Erin McCarley is a singer/songwriter who has been active in both the Nashville and Hotel Café music scenes. The Universal Republic artist's debut album, *Love, Save The Empty*, was in the top ten on iTunes upon its release. The title track to the album was the featured song in the film *He's Just Not That In To You*. McCarley has toured with Brett Dennen, James Morrison and Mat Kearney.

www.erinmccarley.com

O.A.R.

O.A.R. (short for Of A Revolution) is a popular roots-rock band. Having sold out Madison Square Garden, the band is best known for its live shows and its multi-platinum selling hit single, *Shattered* (*Turn The Car Around*) as well as its appearances on ABC's nationally televised college football games and Blackberry commercials.

www.ofarevolution.com

Chris Trapper

Chris Trapper began his career as the front man for The Push Stars, who later signed to Capitol Records. Trapper has written songs that have been placed in *There's Something About Mary*, *The Devil Wears Prada*, and *August Rush* (in which his song, *This Time*, was the lead track to the Grammy nominated soundtrack). He has performed for the United Nations and has won two SoCan Awards for his songwriting work with Great Big Sea. According to Rob Thomas, Chris Trapper writes “the kind of music that songwriters love.”

www.christrapper.com

Marti Dodson

Marti Dodson began her music career as the lead singer of the pop-rock band, Saving Jane. Known for their Top 40 hit, *Girl Next Door*, Saving Jane was signed to Toucan Cove, a Universal Records label. Dodson is now a member of the country group, Union Rose Band, and is currently writing material for a new record.

www.unionroseband.com

Derek Webb

Derek Webb first gained fame as a member of the popular Contemporary Christian band, Caedmon's Call, and later for his solo career. Webb is a leader in the modern digital music business. He was named a visionary and one of the Top 100 Indie Artists of the Past 15 Years by *Performing Songwriter*. He is one of the founders of NoiseTrade.com and was one of the first artists ever to give away full records for free in exchange for information.

www.derekwebb.com

CHAPTER 1

THE STATE OF THE MUSIC INDUSTRY

"For a decade, analysts have been hyperventilating about the demise of the music industry. But music isn't going away. We're just moving out of the brief period—a flash in history's pan—when an artist could expect to make a living selling records alone."

Damian Kulash, Jr., Guitarist for OK GO
(Dec. 17, 2010, *Wall Street Journal*)

* * *

We aren't going to sugar coat it. Having a career as a musician will not be easy. Let's look at the numbers.

The worldwide sales of recorded music totaled $26.9 billion in 1999. In 2009, that figure was $17 billion. And the recorded music that is actually purchased is increasingly intangible. In the U.S., fifty percent of all sales were digital in 2009.

In 2009, there were 105,000 new albums released. Of those, only 6,000 releases sold more than 1,000 units in the first year. Those are not great numbers if you are planning to release one of the 105,000 albums.

As you can see, the sale of recorded music has declined substantially over the past few years. People still love music. It's just that they are less willing to pay for music than they have ever been.

Essentially, the demand for legitimately purchased recorded music has decreased. On the other hand, there have never been as many talented artists putting out records as there are today.

There are a couple of reasons for the overflow of musical talent this millennium. First, the cost of recording has decreased. It used to cost at least tens (sometimes hundreds) of thousands of dollars to make a record. Now, everyone either knows someone with a recording studio or owns GarageBand, Pro Tools or similar recording software.

In the history of mankind it has never been easier to record music. This is both a positive and a negative development. The barriers to entry are lower, but the sheer glut of competition is enormous.

Nashville singer-songwriter Dave Barnes suggests that the ubiquity of these tools has created an uncommon paradigm in music careerism.

"There aren't many jobs in America or in the world where, as in music, it's not really known how you get there." And even as the tools now available—such as social media and the ease of creating and distributing recordings—become ever more accessible, it is increasingly less evident how they should be utilized effectively by career-minded musicians.

"Let's say really good sharp shooters, guys who have a gift . . . you put an ace of spades on top of a fence, sideways, a mile away and a guy can hit it," continues Barnes. "It takes certain people to be able to do that. But with MySpace, everybody's was given a sniper rifle. Just because you've got a gun, that doesn't make you someone who is a good shooter."

Another factor leading to more music is the culture. The new generation is the Facebook generation. We want to express ourselves instantly. We want feedback right away about what other people think of our little thoughts. There is a culture of over-expression of self, bordering on narcissism. Everyone wants to express themselves and, better yet, get rich and famous doing it.

But, don't let the abundance of musical talent force you to put away your guitar case. Just understand that even if you are, by all accounts, extremely talented, you are still facing an uphill battle with many other musical studs climbing the same hill. Know that no one is going to come to your local open mic night and sign you to a million dollar record deal. Those days are over (if they ever existed).

While there have never been more people trying to make a living playing music, there are also more opportunities now than there ever were before, especially if you are trying to build a fan base.

People will always love great music. Songs that listeners connect with in a meaningful way will always be a hot commodity. There will always be room for more great music.

Don’t give up. Just understand what you are getting in to. The music business is seeing the greatest shift since the creation of recording technology. This paradigm shift is beyond the scope of previous developments, such as the introduction of the CD format or the debut of MTV. Having a career in music will be a legitimately and substantively different operation from now on then it has been for the last century.

Don't build your expectations or assumptions on the old (and now defunct) paradigm. Looking toward the future and being open to the development of a new system is key to adapting and thriving in whatever shape the music “industry” takes.

Remember that before recorded music, professional musicians made their livings on patronage, usually on behalf of large institutions such as the Church or governments. Record labels and other music industry institutions leveraged the patronage of fans to support musicians. Corporate sponsors and marketing professionals may be next.

Keep an open mind and be willing to accept change. You have no other choice.

CHAPTER 2

TALENT

When was the last time you bought a product that you knew was really, really bad solely because the package was nice and the marketing campaign was appealing?

Sure, the branding makes a difference, and the advertisements help you remember a product while you're perusing the aisles. But more likely than not, the last time you picked up a six-pack of Budweiser at the local grocery, you did so because you knew what to expect from your purchase. You knew that you liked the taste and experience of drinking a Bud.

Having talent is as central to a successful career as a musician as having a good product is to running a successful company. In fact, more or less, talent *is* your product. Your fans will buy your talent in a roundabout way, either by paying to see you perform or, if you're lucky (at least these days), by purchasing a recorded version of your songs. In essence, what they're buying is *you*. So you'd better be good at being you.

This is not to say that you should forgo a career in music if your voice doesn't sound exactly like Whitney Houston. One of the fantastic competitive advantages you have as a human is that your DNA isn't exactly the same as any other human. You can't be just like anyone else, and no one else can be exactly like you.

Discover And Nurture Your Core Capability.

Unless your career goal is to be an Elvis impersonator, understand what your *unique* talent is and focus your energy on maximizing your talent capital and sharpening your skills. Not everyone is the best singer, the best guitar player, the greatest composer, or the most clever lyricist. You are likely very good at one thing, and can build supporting skills around that main talent.

The business community refers to this as your "core capability," and being able to direct your energy toward this is vital to your professional progress. Not understanding what your talent is and maximizing that talent is like starting a business without a product or service to offer. You wouldn't launch a business without a product. And you can't attempt to launch a career in music without an understanding of *your* product: your talent.

Many successful musicians started careers with passion and drive, but without a true understanding of their unique talent. Jerry DePizzo of O.A.R. admits that he began like so many other musicians, with a deep but focus-less passion.

"For as long as I can really remember, the one centralized theme for me was that I wanted to play music. I never thought it was a career or anything. I just thought it would be cool to play music, mainly guitar. I had an uncle who played me *Eruption* by Eddie Van Halen when I was a kid, *Beat It* by Michael Jackson. Hearing that for the first time seriously knocked me out. It completely floored me, from a very young age. So, I thought, I just want to do that."

DePizzo relates that later a focus emerged around his "core capability" of being a saxophone player that allowed him to contribute to the unique sound that defines O.A.R.

"I know saxophone got me to where I am today and that's what I'm known for and really what I do. But, at first I just wanted to play music," says the sax-rocker.

Focus on defining and maximizing your unique talent before you spend your hard-earned time and money launching a music career without a direction. It will pay off in the long run.

How Good Is Good Enough?

Now let us pose a question: who is the better guitar player – Eric Clapton or Jimi Hendrix?

The answer, at least so far as your musical career is concerned, is that *it doesn't matter*. Both are objectively talented musicians. Whether either one's style is subjectively better is irrelevant to their success as musicians. In order to launch a career in music, there is a minimum threshold point of objective "goodness" that you must reach.

If it is objectively recognizable to everyone that you can't hold a tune or play an instrument, it is pretty darn unlikely that you will be able to convince others to invest in your career, either professionally or consumptively. We won't say this doesn't ever happen, but the laws of probability are not in your favor.

So, in the end it doesn't matter if you prefer Eric Clapton to Jimi Hendrix or John Mayer to Jason Mraz. All of the aforementioned artists are undeniably, objectively talented. They are all “good enough,” and to launch your career, you, too, need to be good enough.

“Talent wins, period,” confirms Nashville singer-songwriter Dave Barnes. “If it comes down to all other things being equal, talent is the factor that trumps all else.”

As Dave explains it, talent is the foundation upon which everything else in your career is built.

“You build a brand on your talent, and from there, you release numerous other 'products.' So you go from 'I'm a singer-songwriter' to ‘I'm an actor,’ to ‘I work in the social atmosphere,’ to ‘I start a philanthropy,’ or ‘I start a clothing line,’ or ‘I have a talk show or an online media presence.’ Your talent becomes a brand, and people now subscribe to *you.* Your role as a talent is to hook [consumers] on to you.”

Ultimately, music is art. There is a minimum level of skill required to “make it.” However, no one will ever have the final say as to whether an individual artist is good enough. Keep working and practicing. In the end, if you, as an artist, can get fans, then you have passed the talent threshold.

QUICK TIPS

- Play with people who are better than you. They will challenge your assumptions about your talent, and give you a yardstick against which to measure your abilities.

- Focus on identifying your core musical capability and spend the majority of your initial effort in cultivating that capability as your main product.

- Along the way, utilize the opinions of people you trust to help you understand what your musical core capability is and use their objective opinions to gauge the improvements you make in developing your talent.

- Accept that there is a minimum threshold point of objectively recognizable talent. Endeavor to cross that threshold point in your own unique manner.

- Your talent *is* your product! Identify your product. Always work to be as good at providing that product as you can. Promote your career by promoting your product. Be great at being you!

CHAPTER 3

GEOGRAPHY

It is no secret that most popular (read: Top 40, Country, and Hip-Hop) music is recorded in concentrated geographic locations. Nashville is home to the overwhelming majority of Country and Christian music. Los Angeles and New York host most of the Rock, Pop, and Hip-Hop music sessions. Of course, there are other genre-specific scenes all around the world.

There is a common belief among up and coming artists from areas outside of the big three Music Cities that geography plays a key role in success. But is success in music as easy as simply packing up the car and getting a minimum wage job in a music town, then waiting to get discovered in a coffee shop or rock club?

The answer: it depends on who you ask and what you want to do.

Being A Big Fish In A Small Pond

Derek Webb started his music career as a guitarist in Houston, Texas playing with a group of friends, that eventually became Caedmon's Call, one of the must popular Contemporary Christian bands of the last fifteen years. After about a decade with Caedmon's Call, Derek embarked on a solo career as a singer-songwriter and relocated to Nashville.

Despite being a current Nashville resident, success as an artist is not dependent upon geography, says Webb.

"When you are first starting, it is better to be a big fish in a small pond. I recommend against anyone moving to Nashville to get into music, out of one side of my mouth. Because everyone in town, from the guy who delivers my mail to the guy who makes my latte, has a publishing deal. I didn't move to Nashville for music. I moved there chasing a girl (his wife, and fellow singer/songwriter, Sandra McCracken)."

"But, out of the other side of my mouth," Webb continues, "I will say that the indie music community in Nashville is a really small community. The people we wind up working with, or touring with, or having play on records with us aren't some top dollar musicians that everyone knows. They are our friends. They are people who we like to hang out with and drink wine on our porch with."

Based upon his own experience in Nashville, there is a difference between the advice that Webb would give to a person seeking to develop a career as an artist by building a fan base and a person seeking to attract the eyes of the recording industry, whether as an artist, session musician or an engineer or producer.

"When people say, 'how would I become a drummer in Nashville and play on your record?' I say, 'Come live in my neighborhood *forever* and be my friend. Be a part of our community.' Those are the people who are getting in. It's a very inbred little community, in a good way. We all have home studios. For example, Will Sayles, this genius drummer who has played on almost all of my records, lives five minutes from me. So, I'll say 'Hey Will, come play some drums.' Proximity is pretty major in that regard."

Webb summarizes his conflicted feelings by saying that moving to a Music City might be a good idea at some point.

"Coming to Nashville eventually could be a great thing, but doing it to get discovered is like being a needle and jumping into a haystack. You are not going to get discovered, unless something really crazy and special happens. Don't stake your career on something crazy happening. Caedmon's Call made it because we were in Houston and there was no one doing what we were doing in Houston."

"If you are doing something well and in a self-sustaining way, people are going to notice. I would rather see someone have a hometown and have fans there. Have a city that is a home base for you. Nashville is not a home base for anybody. That is the thing that sucks about being in Nashville. Everybody has their arms folded with their heads cocked to the side because they are either a critic or are looking at you like you are competition. Be in a place to be under the radar long enough to figure out what you are doing and do it well."

Needles Jumping Into Haystacks

Fellow singer/songwriter Griffin House has a different set of experiences from which to give advice about the importance of geography to a developing artist.

"I think it was really important for me to move to Nashville when I first started because I needed to make connections. But, at a certain point, you make connections, and there are really not that many more that you need to make. You just need to start making great records and keep going and keep working hard. I think you can do that from anywhere."

House moved to Nashville soon after graduating college from Miami University (Ohio). His story seems to be the kind that Derek Webb cautions is unlikely. House moved to Nashville without really having any connections and got a job working for minimum wage on Broadway, the main tourist thoroughfare, in Nashville. When he made friends in Nashville, House made the right friends, which eventually sent him on his current career path. Fellow Nashville residents Marc Broussard and Dave Barnes are part of the story of Griffin House's music career.

"I got a call from a lady at Island/Def Jam records named Diana Fragnito. She was meeting with another artist in Nashville, a friend of mine named Dave Barnes. He was up there for a meeting with her because she had just signed Marc Broussard to Island/Def Jam and so Dave was up there probably meeting to try to get a deal."

"Dave gave her my record in the meeting! He just decided, 'Hey, this is a friend that I believe in. You should listen to his music.' So she called me and flew me up there. I kind of owe a lot to that guy because he opened up a bit of a buzz for me at a time when I needed a door to be opened."

Of course, geography alone is not responsible for Griffin House's career. Nevertheless, had House not moved to Nashville, he would not have met Dave Barnes and Marc Broussard at a time in their own careers when they had the ability to help him.

Dave Barnes, whose tip led to House's first open door, also benefited from the convergence of people and place. "I spent a month at a Young Life camp, and there was a guy there named Bebo Norman, who was just really gracious with his time during that month, and he was the one who introduced me to [record producer] Ed Cash. When Ed was playing a show in Knoxville, I introduced myself, and after that meeting, we stayed in touch while he was still living in Charlotte.

"He was coming to Nashville once or twice a season, and so when he'd come to Nashville, he'd call me and we'd get together and catch up. At this time, I was at college [at Middle Tennessee State University] and playing coffeehouse shows, mostly just for my friends. And then a couple of years later, he said, 'I'm moving, I'd love for you to work for me for a while, help me get everything together,' and I spent six months there, during which we really got to know each other. That got me to Nashville, and at the end of my time there, in 2001, we recorded an E.P., and then [Matt] Wertz asked me to start playing shows and that's when things really took off.

After making these initial connections, Barnes' community was largely responsible for the various open doors that he encountered. After his relationship with Cash resulted in a record, Barnes was able to book gigs and find consistent work playing shows and selling his music.

"I was busy, I wasn't killing it, but I was definitely booking a lot of shows," he says. In doing so, his community expanded to include Marc Broussard, whose aforementioned suggestion of Barnes to label A&R executives kick-started an opportunity to go after an even wider audience base.

Another example of geography leading to relationships leading to success is Erin McCarley.

"I got a guitar and I moved to Nashville right after college. Still, I was just a singer. I just went to a community where there was a network and where people have done it a million times before. There was a formula set up. Initially, I wanted to quit college two years in and go to Nashville. I knew one person in the industry through church or something. I don't even remember what it was. But, that's why it was Nashville and not L.A. or New York."

Once in Nashville, the now Universal Republic artist began meeting people in town and plugging in to the local Nashville music scene. She eventually met the wife of Jodi Williams, a music publisher, while working in a furniture store. The relationship with Williams led to several other relationships with key figures in Nashville and with A&R people throughout the music industry.

Eventually, when McCarley was given an opportunity to showcase at South By Southwest, she sent an email to all of the music industry people she had met in Nashville to tell them about her showcase. She was signed to a major record label deal soon after. Much like Griffin House, McCarley's talent and personality were largely responsible for her success. Still, she never would have met the influential music industry people whom she met without being in Nashville.

The Recording Industry Lives In Music Cities.

For country singer, Johnny Lee, who became one of the first country/pop crossover artists with his hit song, *Lookin' For Love*, location is important, especially for songwriters who don't have the option of directly appealing to the general public to make fans.

"I don't think you have to live in Nashville. Although, you are a lot closer to work if you do," says Lee. "I actually think it is important to at least be close. If you go to Nashville, that is where all the songwriters are. You've got to go there and get locked in and make new friends and learn how they do this. Although, when I lived in Nashville, I got less done than when I didn't because I got taken for granted for living there for awhile. But, for somebody starting out, it is important to be at least close. You need to be where the business is."

O.A.R. saxophonist, Jerry DePizzo, believes that living in a Music City can be important for session musicians, but is not as important today for artists. Location, however, is important.

"I imagine being close [to a Music City] helps. It didn't help us. It didn't hurt us being in Ohio. It helped that we played music that college students gravitate towards and we played in a place where there are a lot of colleges. So, if you want to be in Country music, do you have to move to Nashville? No. But, your chances of being discovered by industry people are much greater if you do."

"You fly to New York to sign a record deal or meet with labels. You fly to L.A. to meet with booking people. That is not going to change. But, what I have noticed about those areas, L.A., New York, Nashville, the talent pool is far deeper. The best player in Columbus would go to L.A. and be an okay guy. Paul Brown, a guy in Columbus, is an unbelievable guitar player. If he goes to New York, he is an average session dude. If you go to L.A., New York, or Nashville, you are where the action is, but there is a lot more competition," says DePizzo.

Another Columbus, Ohio resident, Saving Jane's Marti Dodson says that living in a Music City is not critical to success, but may be a good idea. The *Girl Next Door* singer and songwriter began her career in the Midwest.

“I did it without moving. But, it is certainly not the speedy route. It is easier to make connections and contacts when you live in a city that is music based. It is not critical, but it is helpful.”

To self-made indie artist Brad Skistimas of Five Times August, Music Cities represent the music industry, which is not necessarily required to start a career in music, but is helpful once you have a career.

“I would say living in a Music City doesn’t matter. I grew up in Flower Mound, Texas, a suburb of Dallas. I started developing a following online. We came to Nashville because there is no industry in Dallas. Everyone that I talk to is in L.A., New York or Nashville. I came here to be closer to business. I didn’t come here to break in to the industry. It is great to be here for networking purposes.”

“Everyone that I meet knows someone who knows someone. But how often does that really work? No one ever says ‘I met someone who knows someone, and now I am on the cover of Rolling Stone.’ It depends on what you want to pursue. If you are pursuing a record label, you need to be in Nashville because there are record label people. We are pursuing building a fan base. Nashville is not necessarily the place for us.”

Chris Trapper, frontman of Boston-based pop-rock band, The Push Stars, agrees with Skistimas.

"It depends on what you want to do. If you want to be a session player, then you probably need to live in New York, L.A., or Nashville because those are the only places where enough records are made that there is a volume of work to make a living. If you want to be an engineer, you can live in Cleveland, but you have to realize that you won't get the biggest projects. You might be doing a session of some lady from the suburbs singing Barbara Streisand karaoke covers. As a songwriter, you can live anywhere. The key is that you have to meet people and get out and play and develop fans," says Trapper.

Should You Move?

There is a consensus opinion among the artists interviewed for this book about the benefits and detriments of living in a Music City. There is some debate, however, about whether the detriment or benefit weighs heavier at the start of a career.

We believe that it all comes down to who your audience is and what your goals are. If your goal is to get signed by a major label *without first developing a fan base*, you *should* move to a Music City. That is the place where you are far more likely to get signed because that is where almost all of the industry decision-makers live.

On the other hand, if your goal is to build a fan base from the ground up (or if you already have some regional buzz) you should stay away from the Music Cities. It is much easier to build a fan base in Nantucket than in Nashville.

QUICK TIPS

You should move to Nashville, New York, or Los Angeles for the following reasons:

- If you are a session musician and want to make records, there is far more significant and lucrative work.
- There are numerous great musicians with whom to record and perform.
- If your goal is to appeal to the recording industry, that is where they are located.
- It is easier to make friends with people who can help you in your career in Music Cities.

You should not move to Nashville, New York, or Los Angeles for the following reasons:

- Competition is very, very tough.
- People are jaded with new musicians trying to break in to the industry (because there are so many of them), resulting in it being difficult to build a fan base.
- You can develop a music community anywhere.

CHAPTER 4

BUILDING A FAN BASE

This chapter is dedicated to answering one of the most difficult questions asked by aspiring artists: How do I build up a fan base to be able to have a sustainable career?

The quick answer to that question has four components: (1) Be talented enough to cut through the clutter of life; (2) Invest in your fans; (3) Use technology; and (4) Tour smart.

1. Be Talented Enough To Cut Through Clutter.

The first part is probably the hardest. Fan is short for fanatic, which is "a person with an extreme and uncritical enthusiasm." To build a fan base, you need to be more than just good or great. With so much music competing for attention, you must give people a reason to become a fanatic. You have to stand out.

And you aren't just competing against other music. You are competing against all entertainment options available to your potential fan. Think about the process for a prospective fan to attend a show of a new artist.

First, the fan has to hear the song somewhere, and it has to be *so good* that it cuts through whatever else that person is doing or thinking about, to the point where the person takes enough of an interest in the song to download it or look up the artist. That is no small feat.

Then, the person probably has to find one or two more songs that he or she really likes in order to justify the cost and time commitment of going to a show. And when the artist comes through town opening up for some other artist that the fan doesn't really like or know, the fan has to pay the full ticket price for that artist, after venturing out to a venue or part of town that may be far away from the fan's own neighborhood.

Most people would rather just sit at home and watch television.

Developing artists sometimes talk about how hard it is to get their first one hundred fans, or their first one thousand fans. Here is a better and more attainable goal for getting fans: Try to sell a CD or digital download to someone who is not related to you or to someone who you do not already know.

Your family and friends are (probably) proud of you and will (likely) support you. You are on the right path if you can get a handful of people who are not already invested in you personally to be engaged in your music.

Building a fan base is a difficult thing to do, even if you are signed to a major record label. For Gabe Dixon, whose band was signed to Warner Brothers, he realized that fan relationships were the responsibility of the Artist, not the label.

"We got signed by a guy that produced a record for us. It was great. And then a new president [of the record label] came in and [the guy who signed us] was gone," recalls Dixon. "So he was gone and we didn't have anybody at the label that really gave a shit about us. But we were out on tour, touring the whole country as if we have had some kind of radio single or something, which we didn't. And we kind of abandoned our base a little bit."

Dixon continues, "So I think one of the things that I feel is important for a band is to nurture your base. Because that's the only thing that is truly real. If you have a hit on the radio, but you can't go and play to a big room full of people anywhere, then, enjoy it while it lasts because it's not going to last very long."

Like Dixon, Griffin House relies on the music to do the talking. If the music is good, the songs will do most of the heavy lifting for you when it comes to making fans. "I think some of the songs just work for themselves when I'm not working. Once they are out there, the songs are making fans by just being available when you can't do anything about it," says House.

2. Invest In Your Fans.

Once you have some fans, the second component is to invest in a relationship with those fans.

If you invest in your fans, they will invest in you. Years after his commercial successes from *Urban Cowboy*, including the number one hit *Lookin' For Love*, Johnny Lee understands that his loyal fans have allowed him to continue to make a living.

"Without them, you've got no career. I sit after shows and sign autographs and hug necks and things like that. Had that stopped, I would be a fish out of water right now. I would have had to change careers late in life," says Lee.

O.A.R. initially gained a very loyal fan base without any commercial airplay. Since their platinum hit, *Shattered (Turn the Car Around)*, the band's following has only continued to grow. But, even when O.A.R. signed a record deal with a major label, it was the fans that drew the attention of the label to O.A.R.

"Most people in the industry don't care about any O.A.R. songs, except for maybe *Shattered*. What they want is our audience. We built it from the ground up. Playing shows. Spreading music. Developing communal efforts in pockets around the country. We built ourselves a fan base that allows us to operate outside of the traditional model. We can kind of make our own rules and decide how to do things," says O.A.R.'s DePizzo.

"If you build an audience, everything else will come. If you create an experience live that people come to over and over and over again, the industry will come. It is power in numbers. The record industry had no choice but to gamble on O.A.R. because our numbers were so big," says DePizzo.

Caedmon's Call followed a path similar to O.A.R. by gaining a large fan base established solely on touring without any radio airplay. Caedmon's early success was in 1994 before the widespread use of the Internet.

"People can't imagine a world with no Internet now. But, Al Gore hadn't turned it on yet," recalls Caedmon's Derek Webb.

"Looking back, I don't see how we did it or why. It was really hard. The first bit of marketing, if you want to call it that, was word of mouth. We were college-aged and a lot of people who were our age were able to get us gigs. Eventually, we figured out that we are not distributed anywhere and there is no way for anyone to have heard our stuff or know our stuff. It is hard to make a seven-hour drive to play for fifteen people. You'd have to make four or five trips to that college before you could get a hundred people."

In a bit of foreshadowing for a venture that Webb would later create called NoiseTrade (www.NoiseTrade.com), Caedmon's gave away its music for free to get fans.

"We made cassettes, which were readily copy-able. We put a handful of tunes on it with a little bit of interviews in between with us talking about the tunes. It was like a little sampler. We put them in these little cassette sleeves. Whenever we had a gig at the colleges, we would send a box of these to whoever was promoting the gig and tell them to give them away and tell the people they gave them to to make copies for everybody else."

While Webb and Caedmon's Call did not have the Internet when they built their initial fan base, artists now have a number of technological options at their disposal. Successful artists continue to connect with fans by using technology to reach more people whom the artists would not have been able to reach before.

Marti Dodson is actively involved in the web presence of her band. "I run our websites and our MySpace. I am the one who responds to people. That means something to people if they are reaching out to you because your song affected them," says Dodson.

Similarly, Brad Skistimas of Five Times August spends a large amount of time behind his computer interacting with fans. That level of fan interaction helped him to secure his first fans after he gained exposure from song placements on MTV's *Laguna Beach*.

"I made a huge effort to talk to fans who wrote me and really connect with them. I did this by being accessible to people. Spending five or six hours a day responding to messages. Making sure that everyone who wrote me got a response. Fans love it when you respond. I love doing that," says the Five Times August singer.

3. Use Technology.

Derek Webb has used several types of technology, above and beyond what other artists use, to connect with fans.

After Caedmon's Call, Webb released a solo an album for free in 2006 on his website, giving away around 80,000 downloads and collecting email addresses for his mailing list and zip codes for touring. As a result of this creation, Derek gained more fans for his solo records and, eventually, created the popular free musician download site, NoiseTrade.com.

"[NoiseTrade] has been extraordinary. [After less than] a year in business we are near a million and a half songs total, which for an indie start up that is bootstrapped with no P.R., that is a lot. We have had approximately 175,000 records downloaded. We've paid out more than fifty grand to our artists in tip jar money," says Webb.

Instead of coasting on the success of one of the most popular Christian bands of the 1990s and 2000s in an already niche market, Derek Webb pushed the envelope, both creatively and with industry norms. He would have had a nice solo career without NoiseTrade or giving an album away for free. But now, due to his initiative, his career is likely even better off than it would have otherwise been.

In addition to creating his own technology with NoiseTrade, Webb used Twitter to have more personal connections with fans. Webb loved the television show, *Lost*. While recording an album in 2009, he sent out a tweet with his GPS location and invited the first ten people to come and watch *Lost* with him that night at the studio where his record was being made and listen to some new tracks before they were released.

"The idea came to me because someone said 'Don't update your GPS address because people will be knocking on the ranch door.' I was like, huh? I can't imagine anyone would show up," says Webb. So, I sent out a tweet with the GPS to see if people would come find us. Next thing we know, some dude had driven from College Station and jumped the fence because he didn't know what he was supposed to do. So, he just hung out with us all day while we made the record. We gave him a tour of the ranch. We didn't really think people were going to show up. We were like, what are we supposed to do?"

Eventually, Webb figured out what to do with his new fan-friends. "They came out and we listened to five or six songs on Pro Tools. They watched us record a little. There was a teepee on the ranch and we took them out there and I played one of the songs acoustic for them and we filmed that. So, they will be in our little movie documentary. And we watched *Lost*. We got a bunch of pizzas. They all connected and started following each other on Twitter."

While technology allows new amazing fan interactions with artists that were not previously possible, the best part about technology is that it provides for new ways to invest in fans.

"The technology will keep changing, but all that matters is getting fans. When people ask me what is the first thing you should do as a musician, after writing great songs and being a great performer to have a career. The answer is get fans," says Webb.

Chris Trapper agrees that artists need to keep up with ever-evolving cultural technology. "Myspace has kind of fizzled out and now Facebook is the thing. But real fans will follow you wherever you go. Build fans. Have real interactions with them. That's the difference between me and a big star like John Mayer. I am a person who meets with the fans and talks to them after the show. And, hopefully, they can walk away saying 'this guy is not a dick,'" says Trapper.

4. Tour Smart.

The final component to building fans is to be smart about touring. This includes being thoughtful about which cities to play, when to play them, and what venues to play.

"We were smart about our opportunities. O.A.R. never played a show for five people. It was always packed houses," says DePizzo. "We didn't go and play Columbus one weekend, New York the next, West Virginia the next, and then, Florida. We had a concentrated effort. It was Columbus. Then, Columbus and Athens. Then, Columbus, Athens, Cleveland. Then, Columbus, Athens, Cleveland, Toledo. Then Columbus, Athens, Cleveland, Toledo, Miami (OH). It was an hour radius, then two hours, four hours, and six hours."

Derek Webb echoes DePizzo's sentiment that building a regional fan base through consistent touring is the key to gaining real fans.

"Pick five cities that are close-by and you feel like you could go play shows in. Make it your goal over the next year to get one hundred people in each city. Find a room that is appropriate for the kind of music you play, be it a bar, a college or a church, or whatever it is."

"Develop a relationship with that particular venue. Work all year to get one hundred people in five cities. Once you can do that, work to get two hundred people in five cities. After that, add five more cities and try to get one hundred in those cities. It doesn't take but a few years until you are up to about twenty or thirty cities."

"If you can get two hundred people in thirty cities, and go to all of those cities three times a year, just routing your way around, you will have a vibrant career. You will make plenty of money. Voila! You have a career! You have a job."

Webb's theory makes sense. Let's break down the numbers.

If an artist can play for one hundred people in five cities, assuming a low $5 cover charge that is paid to the artist, then, the artist is making $2,500 in live show revenue. Take that number and make it one hundred people in twenty cities, and play those cities three times per year, then the artist is making $30,000 per year. (100 x $5 = $500 x 20 cities = $10,000 x 3 shows = $30,000.) Once the artist finally reaches the level of two hundred people per show in thirty cities, played three times per year, the gross touring revenue will be at

$90,000! If you change your ticket price to $10, you are looking at $180,000 per year.

Of course, there are expenses associated with touring that must be paid from show revenue. Obviously, the economics of the above illustration work much better with solo acoustic singer-songwriters than with a full band. The point, as made by Webb and DePizzo, is that it is possible to make a living as an artist by starting small with consistent incremental growth.

When The Push Stars first began touring, they were not smart with their opportunities. "We chose our cities randomly. It was not a good strategy. One time, we played a show in Pittsburgh one night and drove back to Boston for an AIDS walk the next day, literally risking our lives to be there on time. It doesn't make sense to play gigs in places where you have not been asked to play," says Trapper.

Now, as a solo artist, Trapper faces the same pitfalls with touring, but has more opportunities because of lower overhead and has learned to tour smarter. "Now, I can play in places where I have never played before, and if you have enough really enthusiastic fans, those fans will bring people. I just had a great show in Hickory, NC and, because there were three or four really big fans who all brought a bunch of people, and the place was packed."

Trapper also knows that a show that seems like it will be a waste of time could lead to something much better for the future. You never know who is in the crowd.

"In San Diego a few years ago, I played a show for about fifteen people, which I thought was a failure. But, I met a lady there who booked me for a house concert the next time I was there. That house concert turned into another even bigger house concert the next time in San Diego. Now, when I play clubs in San Diego, I have a great turn out, based mostly from the house concert buzz. All of that came from the show with just fifteen people," recalls Trapper.

QUICK TIPS

- Be an amazing artist. (See Talent chapter).
- Invest in your fans. Treat them like friends. Be grateful.
- Use whatever technology you feel comfortable using that will allow you to have real interactions with your fans.
- Don't play past the fifteen people who are listening to try to reach the thousands that you wish were listening.

CHAPTER 5

PROACTIVITY

Whether your ultimate goal is to play to packed arenas singing songs that you wrote in your bedroom, or to play bass guitar on a popular Country record written by someone else, one of the keys to a successful music career is personal drive.

Ambitious people have an internal longing to achieve. They share an intrinsic motivation to accomplish their objectives. Make no mistake about it, a career as an artist is a bold path.

Your music will not be heard if you keep your talent a secret. You can't just stand at the door of potential fans and music industry decision-makers. You have to knock. You have to stop making excuses and start making moves.

While ambition alone will not advance a career, a driven personality, when combined with a well-thought out plan, will put you in a position to be more successful than just wandering through life in the music industry. Instead of waiting for something to happen *to you*, you should take Mariah Carey's advice and Make It Happen *for you.*

The artists interviewed in this book all did that in one way or another.

Get Out There And Play!

The first step to being proactive is getting out of your bedroom and performing live. "We had gigs booked before we had a name," says Marti Dodson. "We were pretty much a cover band at first. Our goal was to play covers to make money to fund the recording of originals. We were 75/25 covers at first."

Saving Jane got live experience from playing as a cover band, even before they had written songs of their own. Those cover band gigs led to an opportunity to play at several events sponsored by WNCI, the ClearChannel pop station in Columbus, Ohio. Once the band was connected at WNCI, people at the station introduced the band to the manager of Blessid Union of Souls, who would go on to become the manager for Saving Jane. These connections could not have been made without Saving Jane's early work paying in their dues as a cover band.

Another Columbus, Ohio product, roots-reggae-rock band O.A.R. took their career in their own hands by reaching out to their first fans—friends and fellow students at The Ohio State University—by throwing big house parties where O.A.R. performed.

"When the band first started, they were like the high school band that your friends had. There wasn't a regional or national O.A.R. It was four guys that played their local coffee shop and then went on to college," says O.A.R. saxophonist, Jerry DePizzo.

The sheer volume of shows performed by O.A.R. set them apart and, along with their brand of unique upbeat rock, eventually created a buzz for the band. But, O.A.R. did not wait for an opportunity to open for a national act or to get discovered by a major label. Instead, they created the snowball of momentum with house parties and indie CD releases, which led to an eventual avalanche of O.A.R. becoming a dorm-hold name in Midwest colleges at the turn of the Millennium.

Growing up and living in Boston, Chris Trapper had always wanted a career as an artist. His career began the day that he decided to start playing live. "I started out playing an open mic at a coffee house in Boston that was really a poetry slam place. Then, there was a guy who was a well-known singer/songwriter in Boston who helped me get some gigs at some other places."

Trapper's band, The Push Stars, formed as a result of Trapper getting involved in the local music scene and going to concerts.

"I was at a show at The Middle East in Boston and saw Ryan (MacMillan) playing drums with another band. So I talked to him after the show about playing together some time and it went from there," says Trapper. "Our bass player started out as a session player on our demo. But he sounded so good that we asked him to become a full time member."

The Push Stars management had connections to attorney Rosemary Carroll, who helped shop the band's first record to major labels. They also had a manager who knew The Farrely Brothers, which helped the band get a placement in the film *There's Something About Mary*. While

Trapper recognizes the value of connecting with influencers for an artist, he cautions against thinking about relationships in terms of "networking."

"Take that word '*networking*' and never use it again. Just be real and talk to people and be cool. I can tell when people are being genuine and when they are being opportunistic. Someone like Rob Thomas, who deals with a hundred people a day who want something from him, has an unbelievable bullshit detector. He can tell right away whether someone is genuine. Just be a real person. If you do that, you will meet people," says Trapper.

Don't Make Excuses.

One of the many obstacles faced by artists is lack of passion from those surrounding you. After struggling with his college band to finish a record, Griffin House demonstrated his dedication to a music career when he issued an ultimatum to his bandmates.

"I got really serious about music. I really wanted to do it and try as hard as we could. The band was sort of floundering and I said, 'If we don't have a record recorded by the end of the summer, I'm quitting the band. This is ridiculous,'" says House. "We were spending, like, two or three days a week driving from Cincinnati up to Oxford to rehearse during the summer. So, we were really dedicated, but just not getting anywhere."

After a semester studying abroad in Europe, and still without a record from his college band,

House began recording a solo record. “I did [the record] on a digital 12 track recorder. One of the guys in the band helped me mix it and put it on to CD form. I took it to school and pressed up a bunch of copies and started selling it to all of my friends, guys I knew in fraternities, people in class.”

“Then, I started playing shows out by myself at Miami University. That was my first experience of performing live. I kept doing that and doing that. I kept making recordings and playing as much as I could. Eventually, I moved to Nashville and one thing led to another.”

Instead of letting an excuse dominate his music career, Griffin House took control. If not for his own determination to record his songs and get the music in to the hands of his friends and people at his college, House might have a career in another field. In addition to making his own record and playing solo concerts at Miami University, House took the ultimate leap into the music career and moved to Nashville, without the support of any bandmates. Determination is certainly one of the keys to Griffin House’s success in music.

Another Nashville transplant, Erin McCarley, hit the ground running once she landed in the Music City. Although she didn’t play shows around town right away, her actions were far more effective and lasting than playing at any open mic. McCarley, through a series of acquaintances, first plugged in to a community of kindred artists and built relationships.

"My part-time job helped me to meet people. Right when you are starting [in Nashville], it is good to put yourself in a position of service, whether it is retail or restaurant. It is so cliché, but it is true," says the *Love, Save The Empty* singer.

"I worked at Starbucks. I also worked at this furniture store where a lot of designers came for interior design. All of these wives of music execs in the town were coming through. I met this one wife, who happened to be the wife of a publisher in town, Jodi Williams."

In addition to meeting Jody Williams in Nashville, she met friends who would later introduce her to her eventual record producer, Jamie Kenney, and to another mentor of hers, Kathleen Carey, from Sony Music.

"When I moved to Nashville, I didn't have a place to live. My boyfriend at the time's college friend's brother lived in Nashville. He called him and asked if he knew anyone who needs a roommate. The guy in Nashville's roommate was leaving and there was an extra room in the house. So there were two guys with an extra room, and I moved in. They were part of a group of friends that had a lot of songwriters in the group. In moving in with them, and in hanging with their circle of friends, I met people. And Nashville is small, especially when you start talking music. It all collides. Even with the geography, everybody is within twenty minutes of each other. So, it is really easy to meet people. In Nashville, I was being social and fluttering around."

You heard that right. Her *boyfriend's friend's brother* led Erin McCarley to the group of friends who would introduce her to her record producer and a number of industry people who would build buzz around Erin McCarley, culminating in major labels courting her and ultimately a deal signed with Universal Republic. Erin took a step out of her comfort zone and got to know people in a community of Nashville musicians.

Making It Happen The Johnny Lee Way

The first few opportunities in an artist's career may have to be self-manufactured. However, eventually (and sometimes initially), opportunities present themselves. A successful and proactive artist takes advantage of such chances to be heard, no matter what they may be.

One of the best stories that I have ever heard about an artist creating an opportunity is the story of Johnny Lee.

The country singer was a fan of Mickey Gilley, a well-known country singer, and wanted an opportunity to sit in with Gilley's band. Lee went to a concert of Gilley's and made a risky career calculation that paid dividends.

"I went up to him and I introduced myself to him and said, I know you don't remember me, but I did a TV show with you in Galveston, Texas a while back," says Lee. "I said 'I was on before you. You came on after me. We didn't have time to stick around. We had a job that night. I heard you were up here and I just wanted to come up and say hi and tell you what a great artist I think you are. I've been listening to your playing and singing," Lee told Gilley.

The reality, however, was that Johnny Lee had never played a show with Mickey Gilley. Johnny's story about having previously opened for Mickey Gilley was pure fiction.

"So, instead of me asking Mickey Gilley if I could sit in and sing, and him having the opportunity to say no, I just acted like I knew him. He ended up asking me if I wanted to sit in with the band. I said, 'Sure.' He asked me to sit in with him a few more times. He eventually offered me a job. But, in all reality, I had never seen him before in my life," recalls Lee.

"If I was asking him if I could sit in, then he could always say no. So, I figured that if he thought I was good enough to be on a television show, then maybe he would ask me to play with him. And he did. He was just being courteous. I ended up being the band leader a few months later," says Lee.

You read that correctly.

Johnny Lee wanted an opportunity to get his foot in the door with Mickey Gilley, so he simply lied to Gilley, hoping that the lie would not be spotted and that Gilley would react as Lee expected and ask him to sit in with the band. This hoodwink act of Lee's led to a strong regional country career for several years, and later to a country/pop crossover hit with *Lookin' For Love* and an acting role in *Urban Cowboy* with John Travolta.

This strategy almost certainly would not work today. First, you would not likely have access to the artist. Second, the artist's management would probably immediately Google you to see if you had any credibility.

Still, Lee's story is a good illustration of what it looks like to really want a career, and to create an opportunity for yourself.

Answer When Opportunity Knocks.

Derek Webb's former band, Caedmon's Call, began as a result of the band "chasing down the opportunities at the time," says Webb. "[Bandmate] Cliff [Young's] dad is a big pastor in Texas and they had a full-fledged recording studio in their church and there was a possibility that we could go record some music. Then a friend got us a gig at Rice University. Then, we had a little thing that we pressed onto some cassettes with a few more songs. Then, some other friends got us some gigs at some other colleges in Texas. We started making drives on the weekend. Literally, it was like that," says Webb.

When an opportunity finally presents itself, proactive artists take advantage of the opportunity. Brad Skistimas' music career began with a television placement on the season finale of MTV's popular reality show, *Laguna Beach*.

"The thing about the first MTV placement is that the offers went out to thousands of people. A friend of ours who still lives at home with his parents and has been doing this longer than Brad has got the same email from MTV. The exact same email, word for word. He deleted it because he thought it was a random person asking for a CD," says Skistimas wife and manager, Kelly Vandergriff.

"It just shows you that you have to jump on things as soon as they are presented to you. If you don't, there are a thousand artists, right behind you who will jump on it," says Skistimas.

QUICK TIPS

- Write songs.
- Perform live.
- Attend concerts in your city.
- Make real relationships with other artists whom you admire.
- Do not wait around for someone to discover you.
- Do not make excuses.

CHAPTER 6

PROFESSIONAL SUPPORT

One of the first things that developing artists believe they need to advance their careers is professional support. While music industry professionals are certainly helpful and necessary, bringing them in to the picture is almost guaranteed to use up scarce financial resources. On the other hand, the right personnel at the right time, can be the missing link in an artist's career.

The primary professional support team consists of managers, booking agents, publicists, and attorneys. Before you decide to start shelling out cash to the suits, let's take a look at what the various professional personnel actually do, and the advice our artists have regarding them.

Managers

Using a professional sports metaphor, a manager is the coach of the team. The artist is the owner. The artist sets out the directive and the general direction of what he or she would like to do with their career, while the manager implements strategies to get the job done.

Actual tasks for the manager vary wildly, depending on the goal of the artist. For most new acts, a manager's tasks include press kit creation, assisting with merchandise creation, web site, social media (Facebook, Twitter, MySpace), and booking the artist's first concerts. Typically, a manager receives a percentage (generally ten to twenty percent) of all entertainment-related income from the artist. For that reason (and hopefully because the manager likes the artist's music), a manager is the artist's biggest cheerleader.

An artist should carefully consider (1) if they need a manager, (2) when to have one, and (3) who to hire. The right decisions can create opportunities. The wrong decisions, however, can stop a promising career in its tracks.

According to Chris Trapper, an artist should not hire a manager just because they do not have one.

"Focus on making great music and having a reason for a manager. The Push Stars got a manager when we started to fill up clubs and have people approaching us with business cards at the end of shows that we didn't know what to do with. We didn't get a manager to push us to the next level. You have to create your own motion on the tracks, not expect a manager to take you to the next level. They can help, but not get you there."

Marti Dodson from Saving Jane believes that having a manager is crucial from the get-go. "For me, it was something that was good out of the gate. I didn't have any relationships or know anyone in the industry. If I was doing it again, I would say get a manager immediately," says Dodson, whose band had the assistance of Mark Liggett, an experienced manager with previous major label success.

O.A.R. also had a great management experience. "We were fortunate because we had [lead singer Marc Roberge's] brother, Dave Roberge, at the helm steering the business side of the ship. He was a sharp guy and he learned as trial by fire. He went to Florida. Graduated from Florida in '98. He was working at a job in Vegas. The guys called him at first and asked to help book some shows and look over proposals. Dave left his job and moved back to Florida with his fiancé and future wife and ran O.A.R. out of an apartment in Florida before he got married and moved back to Maryland and eventually to New York."

Although O.A.R. has a very strong manager, DePizzo cautioned against acting too hastily in finding a manager.

"Try to learn and develop and do on your own as much as is possible. Finding the right manager and the right guy for the job is more important than finding a guy to fill the job. I can't tell you exactly when that is, or when it should happen. But, when you are focusing on the business side of things more than you are focusing on the music side of things, and there is someone available that is qualified to do it. I would say that is the time to hire a manager," says the saxophonist for the platinum selling band.

Hiring the right manager does not necessarily mean hiring someone who is well-known or experienced.

"Someone qualified to do it may not be a professional manager at a management company.

It may just be a really sharp buddy of yours. That's what it was for us. The band wouldn't be where it is today if not for David. I sleep pretty well at night when it comes to Dave Roberge. I don't worry about whether this guy is stealing my money or leading us in the right direction. He is fully invested in this. I sleep well at night knowing that I have someone that I trust, and love really, at that position."

"Not everyone is going to have that. But, there may be someone sitting next to you who is a friend of yours that may be just as sharp as someone at a management company. They just may not be as experienced. If they are allotted the amount of time to become experienced and have the drive to grow, that may be a better fit than going and hiring a management team who might push an intern on you to run your band at that point," says DePizzo.

Caedmon's Call also relied on a friend of the band to take care of the management duties. "We had this friend who [singer Cliff Young] had gone to college with named Kirby Trapalino. At the time, Kirby was in school in the Northeast. All that we knew was that Kirby was a smart dude who we liked to hang out with," says Caedmon's Call member Derek Webb.

"Cliff called Kirby on the phone and said 'Hey man. What are you doing?' He said 'I'm going to college.' Cliff said, 'Come back to Texas and manage our band.' Kirby said, 'I don't know anything about managing a band.' Cliff was like, 'Neither do we, but we are doing it now.' Somehow he talked Kirby into moving down to Texas. This was before we were even signed," recalls Webb.

Eventually, Kirby built a distribution network for Caedmon's Call records in local music stores throughout the region. "The network continued to build, even after we were signed. It went on to be Grassroots Music, one of the leading indie distributors in the country. That all came out of a guy who didn't know anything about management or marketing saying 'What do we need?' We need distribution. Let's go do it then. Let's create it. When we approached this blue-collar work, we asked ourselves, what are the major things that need to be done. Kirby did a great job over those years of figuring out what those things were," recalls Webb.

Johnny Lee shared a much different management story. Lee has had very bad experiences with managers. In fact, Lee's first management contract resulted in a lawsuit. "My manager had me under a 99 year contract at 50 percent. That wouldn't have been bad if I had got my 50 percent. But I ended up getting f*cked out of that," says Lee.

"You've got to remember that all my life I have been working to be able to travel the country to play. And now I have the number one record in the country and I'm traveling all over the country. My dreams were coming true. My manager said 'I'm going to make you a millionaire.' I trusted the guy."

"It cost me just about all the money that I had in a bank account to pay lawyers, and I got screwed out of all the songs I had written. I never saw any royalty checks from *Lookin' For Love* or anything like that. I got my songs back that I had written, but by that time, all of my money was gone," laments Lee.

Lee was also burned in his next manager relationship, where his manager took a fee as a booking agent and as a manager, but was not doing any work for Lee. Having been taken advantage of by a manager once before, Lee would not let it stand again.

Lee explained how he resolved the problem.

"I leaped over his desk and told him that I was gonna f*ck him up if he didn't tear up the contract. At that point in my life, I had already been screwed over so bad, that I didn't want to get f*cked again. So, right there and then, he dissolved our contract and I have never had another manager since."

Managers are perhaps the most important type of professional personnel for an artist. Still, artists should carefully consider whether to sign with a manager. If you cannot say that you absolutely trust your manager, then you have not found the right person. It is better to go without a manager than to have the wrong manager.

Booking Agents

Booking agents book live performances for artists. Many new artists are looking for a booking agent, believing that the booking agent can get them the gig that they cannot get. Like managers, booking agents are generally paid on a commission. For this reason, most booking agents will not accept new artists who do not already have a history of selling tickets to shows. The booking agent is not going to make much money unless the agent can successfully book shows, which means that there is already a demand for the artist.

At major booking agencies, such as CAA, William Morris, and Paradigm, a booking agent can assist with playing matchmaker for developing artists to open for a national artist. Still, the major booking agencies are only interested in artists who are either already drawing large crowds or have just signed a major label record deal.

The result of this vicious circle is that the artist himself or the manager usually acts as the booking agent until the artist has an established history.

All of the artists we interviewed said that they did not begin to work with booking agents until they were either on a major label or were already drawing large crowds at their concerts. Securing a booking agent right away is something that almost never happens for an artist. Focus on making great music and building your fan base. The booking agents will eventually seek you out if you really need one.

Publicists

The role of a publicist is just like it sounds. They generate publicity for the artist and, in some cases, help manage public relations. In the past, publicists were part of in-house staffs for record labels. Now, however, there are many excellent publicists that are hired guns who work on a project-to-project basis. Those projects are generally new record releases or tours. Most publicists work on a fee based system (paid up-front). They do not take a percentage of your revenue.

The right publicist for you will have relationships with the media that you are trying to reach as an artist. For example, if you are a jazz crooner, you don't need a publicist who has connections at Heavy Metal magazine. For beginning artists, especially in major cities, the most important media is usually an alternative weekly newspaper. Alt-weeklies generally review and promote new artists, and will provide the early reviews of your music that are needed for the press kit. And remember, the manager frequently fulfills the duties of a publicist at the outset of an artist's career.

Independent artist Brad Skistimas of Five Times August started out doing publicity on his own, and eventually transitioned to hiring a professional publicist. "[At first], I wrote every high school paper, every college paper, every city organization for every show. I would spend half a day just contacting media outlets for one show.

That is how we did things for 3 years," says Skistimas.

Later, when Five Times August became the first unsigned artist to have national distribution in Wal-Mart stores, Skistimas hired an outside publicist and was not pleased with the performance.

"She wasn't necessarily the wrong person, but there was a cheese factor to how she was doing our story. The publicist sent out a press release that said 'Five Times August to Release New Album.' That only works if you are Coldplay or John Mayer. We ended up redoing everything she did. She didn't get us anything. She said that everyone kept saying there is no story. We were like, you are not pitching it right. How about 'Unsigned Artist Gets in to Wal-Mart!'" That was our first experience with a big waste of money."

Five Times August has had good experiences with other publicists. "On the last album, we worked with a great publicist out of New York called Shore Fire. They got me my first live TV appearance on the CBS Early Show. They got us Billboard, Guitar Player, Performing Songwriter, Teen Vogue. They are expensive, but they do the job very well," says Skistimas.

Another strong publicity campaign for Five Times August came through a video publicist. "It was great cheap marketing: $3,000 for a two-month campaign. Our video was added to fifty different retail outlets. The campaign was with HitVideo. That was our number one cheap cost where people came out to shows because they saw a video in some store," recalls Kelly Vandergriff.

Attorneys

Attorneys play two major roles for new artists. First, and most obviously, attorneys provide legal advice and services. The most important legal issues for new artists are legal entity formation, band agreements, copyright registration, and trademark registration. Second, attorneys can connect artists to other professional personnel whom the attorney believes would make sense for that artist.

In some cases, an attorney can refer an artist to a record label's artist and repertoire department (A&R), the department that has the authority to sign new artists to recording contracts. (Note: Beware of attorneys who claim to be able to get you a recording contract if you pay them a fee up-front, especially if they have not heard your music. Those attorneys are almost certainly going to take your money with no real benefit offered.)

The music industry is a complicated one. Music law and all of the copyright issues that are unique to music make it crucial to hire a music attorney – not just a regular attorney – for any legal issue that you may have.

For example, a very smart lawyer who does not practice music law will have no idea what a contract means when it talks about synchronization, derivative, mechanical, and master use licenses. Perhaps more importantly, a non-music attorney will not have a finger on the pulse of the constantly changing music industry norms. Only a true entertainment attorney will know whether certain terms in a contract are a good deal or not.

Johnny Lee, whose legal issues with managers were previously documented, never had an attorney review his contracts. "I wish I would have [had an attorney]. I so recommend it. It is a must. There is so much shit. If I would have known about all that stuff, I might have ended up being an attorney instead of a recording artist," says Lee.

O.A.R.'s DePizzo agrees. "I think anytime you have to sign something, an attorney is a good idea. I don't think you need to have one on your payroll. But anytime you have to sign a contract that binds you to somebody else, you should have an attorney look it over."

Griffin House was forced to hire an attorney when he began being courted by record labels. "I remember talking to Lost Highway and I was excited about that label because, before moving to Nashville, I was a huge Ryan Adams fan, and I was talking to Luke Lewis (the guy who runs Lost Highway) on the phone one day. He said, 'We'd really like to do a deal, but we're not going to do anything until you have a lawyer.' So, then I realized that I needed to find a lawyer," says House.

House's lawyer did more than just review contracts. "He helped me get organized and started. To a degree, he was a manager for me before I had a manager."

QUICK TIPS

- Determine if you really need a manager. If you do, make sure you trust your manager.
- Have clear goals and responsibilities for your manager.
- Consider hiring a smart and motivated friend without a music background to be your manager.
- Give your publicist a story that resonates.
- Hire a publicist with a known track record.
- Never sign any legal document without having an entertainment attorney review it.

CHAPTER 7

LIGHTNING STRIKES

The subject of how career artists got their first big break is always fascinating. It piques the interest of non-artists because everyone loves a good old-fashioned rags-to-riches story. And, of course, people who are trying to follow in the footsteps of those who have already "made it" want to see what has worked for others so that they can try to replicate the model.

In the past, the cliché for a big break story was getting heard by an A&R representative for a major record label, who then offered the artist a high-dollar recording contract. Then, everyone lives happily ever after with piles of money like Scrooge McDuck.

That still happens. Rarely. But it does still happen. When it happens, it is never quite as simple as the short version of the story sounds. Even if an artist is discovered by an A&R representative in a random bar, chances are that there were other circumstances that led to that seemingly serendipitous encounter.

Without a doubt, there are pivotal moments that take an artist's career to the next level or give an artist their first big break. Because those moments seem to come out of nowhere and appear to be unpredictable and random, we call those moments "lightning strikes" moments.

Every artist that we interviewed had a first big break. In some cases, that big break changed everything. In other cases, there was slow and steady growth with small break after small break. This chapter gives a quick summary of how each artist that we interviewed made a career in music.

You can't make lightning strike, but you can do things to make it more likely that when lightning does strike, it will hit you. That is the goal of this book – to give you a glimpse behind the curtain to see what really happens so that you can narrowly tailor your efforts to get the best results.

People say it isn't what you know, but who you know that matters. The reality is that both are important. In the music industry connections are king. But, as you will see with the stories of Griffin House, Saving Jane, and Erin McCarley, being "connected" doesn't mean that you are making shady deals in back rooms. It means that you know people who are in the music business and they think you are amazingly talented and will fill an underserved niche in the market. Also, and of equal importance, they like you and are willing to help.

You can't make lightning strike. But meeting the right people and making those connections in the right way makes it more likely that lightning will strike. When it does, you, like the artists we interviewed, better be ready to seize the opportunity.

Griffin House

Without knowing any music industry people in Nashville, Griffin House moved to the Music City right after college. He worked a job on Broadway, a primary tourist area of Nashville, for minimum wage. When he wasn't working, He was going out to clubs and venues in Nashville and quickly made friends and connections in Nashville by volunteering to open for headlining acts for free.

Griffin's network of musical friends eventually led to him being discovered by major label A&R departments, at the recommendation of his friends. First, Island/Def Jam Records pursued him. Then, other major labels approached Griffin after learning about Island/Def Jam's interest in him.

The initial Island/Def Jam pursuit of Griffin was a direct result of two of House's friends who are strong career artists themselves: Marc Broussard and Dave Barnes.

"Diana Fragnito from Island/Def Jam was meeting with another Nashville artist friend of mine, Dave Barnes. She had just signed another friend of ours, Marc Broussard, to Island/Def Jam. Dave was up there meeting with Island/Def Jam to try to get a deal and he gave her my record in the meeting! He decided 'this is a friend that I believe in and you should listen to his music.' So, then Island/Def Jam called me and flew me up to New York. I kind of owe a lot to that guy because he opened up a bit of a buzz for me at a time when I needed a door to be opened."

Griffin House moved to Nashville, where he happened to befriend Dave Barnes and Marc Broussard, and then Dave Barnes brought a Griffin House CD with him to an interview when Barnes got his big break with a major label and gave it to the label rep while they were talking about signing Barnes. Although House did not ultimately sign with Island/Def Jam, the door pried open for House by Dave Barnes led to a contract with Nettwerk and a vibrant career for House.

Dave Barnes

Following the previous story, we see how lightning can strike due to the company you keep. For Barnes, lightning struck in two separate but major instances, both of which revolved around relationships that ultimately created major opportunities.

"I spent a month at a Young Life camp, and there was a guy there named Bebo Norman, and that was right when I was starting to get serious about songs, and songwriting. And he was just really gracious with his time during that month, and he was the one who introduced me to Ed Cash. That got me to Nashville, and at the end of my time working with him, in 2001, we recorded my songs, and then [Matt] Wertz asked me to start playing shows and that's when things really took off."

Shortly after launching himself in earnest with the connections and assistance of Norman and Cash, Barnes' reputation was spreading throughout the Nashville music community. One of the musicians who became familiar with Barnes' music was Marc Broussard, who was on the verge of signing with a major record label imprint and was already touring heavily. The first time Barnes met Broussard was at a show when Broussard performed one of Barnes' songs.

From there, Broussard and Barnes became friends and colleagues, and shortly thereafter, Broussard advocated for Barnes to Island Def/Jam. The culmination of these lightning strikes moments meant that Barnes had developed a partnership with Ed Cash, who became his producer and with Broussard, who advocated for and ultimately helped Barnes build buzz among major record labels years in advance of Barnes signing a record deal with Razor and Tie.

Saving Jane

Saving Jane's Marti Dodson began her rise to commercial radio success by starting a cover band with a guy she met at a party while at Ohio State University. One of the band members had a connection to the local pop radio station, WNCI. WNCI then booked Saving Jane as a cover band to play for tailgate parties. The station director at WNCI liked Saving Jane and introduced them to Mark Liggett, the former manager for Blessid Union of Souls. Mark became their manager and had a relationship with Toucan Cove, the record label who eventually signed Saving Jane.

The Saving Jane Drummer knew WNCI personnel, who knew Mark Liggett, who knew people at Toucan Cove. That seems like a lot of people to lead to a record deal. But singer/songwriter Erin McCarley had even more people helping her along the road that led to her record deal with Universal Republic.

Erin McCarley

The popular story of Erin McCarley's major-label signing is that she played a showcase at the South By Southwest Music Conference and was noticed by an A&R guy who was impressed. That part of the story is true, but there were a lot of things that led up to that moment.

McCarley moved to Nashville after graduating from Baylor University in Waco, Texas. She moved in to an extra room in her "boyfriend-at-the-time's college friend's brother's house." She became friends with a lot of the same people who her new roommates knew. Many of those people happened to be songwriters and people in the music industry. Out of that original group of friends, McCarley was introduced to Kathleen Carey, a Vice President at Sony Music and Jamie Kenney, the executive producer of her first record.

Erin got a job at a furniture store in Nashville to make money while pursuing her music career. One day while working, she met the wife of music publishing executive Jody Williams. Jody's wife really liked Erin, without even hearing her music, and introduced her to Jody.

Jody helped Erin get in to singing country demos and introduced her to a lot of people in town, including the head of Universal South, Tony Clark. She even had a meeting with Tony Clark, expecting to get signed.

McCarley recalls, "I went to Tony Clark's office, played him the stuff and thought 'Is this gonna be my moment to get a record deal?' He looked at me and was like, 'I love your voice. It is not country at all. Why are you doing this?'

After being rejected from major labels as a country singer, Erin moved to San Diego. "I worked at this little boutique on the beach. Women would come in and we would get to talking and they would ask 'What do you do other than this?'" says McCarley. "I would say 'music.' But, I wasn't going home at night doing anything that had to do with music. I would wake up at 4 A.M. thinking why am I not doing music."

Eventually, after some inspiration from Kathleen Carey of Sony Music, McCarley started writing consistently in San Diego. "I really isolated and stayed disciplined. On days when I didn't work, I didn't get out of my pajamas. I would just stay at home and write from eight to eight."

Then, Erin made it known to her friends in Nashville that she was looking to make a record from all of these new songs that she had been writing. She was introduced to Jamie Kenney, who produced and recorded her first record. Erin and Jamie recorded a full album of material that would eventually be her first record, *Love, Save The Empty*.

Erin knew that she wanted to play at South By Southwest, but she did not have a showcase scheduled there. So, she used her connection at BMI, Jody Williams, to get on the BMI showcase. Then, she emailed every contact that she had made during her time in Nashville. She had enough people in her contact list to create buzz among A&R reps at the showcase.

After a great performance at the BMI South By Southwest showcase, Erin was courted by several major labels and her star began to rise immediately.

"It really was like the dream of South By Southwest. After that night, my future manager (who also manages John Mayer) called and said let's meet. We met at 1:30 in the morning at the Driscoll Hotel. Everyone was partying and he was stone cold sober. I was like 'What am I doing? This is crazy. I don't understand what is going on.' He was like, 'Hey, come to New York.' Then, Universal Republic was like, 'Hey, come to New York.' Then, Columbia was like 'Hey, come to New York.' About a month and a half of New York, L.A., Chicago, I flew back and forth and even met Rick Rubin in Malibu at his house."

While Erin McCarley's performance at South By Southwest was important, the showcase would not have happened without Jody Williams. No one would have come to that showcase without the years of contacts that she made in Nashville. She would not have drawn attention and created buzz to attract A&R reps without Jamie Kenney's help on the record. All of these things combined to create the perfect set of circumstances for Erin McCarley to sign a major label recording contract.

While Erin McCarley, Saving Jane, and Griffin House were helped by their connections, Johnny Lee took a bolder path to stardom.

Johnny Lee

Johnny had been playing in Galveston, Texas with his band. He knew that Mickey Gilley was a big-star in Houston. (This was during the late 1970s when there were truly big stars in regional music and radio stations were not all controlled by a few companies playing the same music.) One night, Lee went to Houston to try to meet Gilley and get an invitation to sit in with Gilley's band. Lee told Gilley that he had opened up for him in Galveston. But there is a twist in Lee's story. It wasn't true.

"Instead of me asking him if I could sit in and sing, and him having the opportunity to say no, I just acted like I knew him. He ended up asking me if I wanted to sit in with the band. I said, 'sure.' He asked me to sit in with him a few more times. He eventually offered me a job. But, in all reality, I had never seen him before in my life, " recalls Lee.

Johnny Lee was able to capitalize on the regional spotlight that Mickey Gilley was in. Then, he parlayed his regional success in to national success when Irving Azoff (who was managing the Eagles at the time) heard Lee singing and asked him if he wanted to sing some songs in a movie. The movie was *Urban Cowboy* with John Travolta. Lee's song Lookin' For Love became the number one pop hit in the country.

There were certainly other factors leading to Johnny Lee's success. However, ultimately, the largest single factor is that he told an exaggerated untruth to a country star to get ahead. And it worked.

Five Times August

Sometimes a "lightning strikes" moment is truly the turning point in a career. It's an event that will change an artist's life. For Five Times August, an email from a music supervisor did just that.

"I remember getting this email that said "MTV music supervisor" in the subject line and reading it and thinking 'Holy Crap!' I was like 'Who is this guy?' All that it said is "Interested in getting your music on a MTV show? Can I get a free copy of a cd?" I was like, this guy either just wants a free copy of a CD, or it could be legit. If anything, I would lose a buck and a half on a CD, recalls Skistimas from Five Times August.

"So I sent it to him and he used a song called *Better With You* on the first season of Laguna Beach. It was 90 seconds out of a 30 minute episode, which is a long time. It was a montage, that was pretty much a music video for the song. My first placement was 90 seconds. At the end of the episode it said 'You just heard Five Times August.' At the end of the next week, my iTunes sales went up. My MySpace listens skyrocketed."

The morale of the story from Five Times August is not to put your music up on MySpace and hope that a miracle happens. (Although, that is apparently possible). The key to Five Times August's success was Skistimas's readiness to capitalize on the strike of lightning when it hit. Skistimas has made a career out of a single television placement, and managed to get more than fifty additional placements, by interacting with fans and placing the MTV logo on every bit of press that he did. In fact, Skistimas later found out that one of his friends received the same email, but didn't respond to it. When your time comes, you have to be ready.

O.A.R.

For O.A.R. there was not a single moment that had a large impact on the career path of the band.

DePizzo says, "There was never a point when one day we were X and the next day we were 10X. It was really a steady gradual build for years and years and years. There are certain things that have helped. If there was one, it was that when the band recorded the first record, they recorded *Crazy Game of Poker*. That was the song that caught people's ear and got them in to the music. Having [our manager] Dave involved was a big part of it too."

O.A.R. also benefitted from coming on to the scene at the height of Napster and from colleges providing high-speed Internet to students. The technology, which is now a double-edged sword, really helped O.A.R. get its music out to fans.

But, remember, there were a lot of other bands that had the same technological benefits as O.A.R. who are no longer playing music. For O.A.R., many factors, including live performances, strong songwriting, and wise management, led to the band's sustained success.

Caedmon's Call/Derek Webb

Caedmon's Call's first big break was when the band was heard by the son of Wayne Watson, an artist with a production deal with Warner Alliance. Watson's son, who was in college at the time, passed the Caedmon's Call demo along to his dad. Watson was immediately interested in the band and helped them land a record deal.

Thanks to the work and guidance of their manager, Caedmon's Call was touring regionally in tour busses at the time Watson's son heard their demo. It was the band's positioning of themselves to be hit by lightning by their constant touring that resulted in the opportunity.

Another break for Caedmon's Call was the recording studio that they had access to in a large church, where one of the band member's fathers was the preacher. If they didn't have a record and if they weren't touring, Watson's son never would have heard the record and passed it on to his dad.

Chris Trapper/The Push Stars

Chris Trapper has been the front man of an up and coming band, been signed to Capitol Records, left Capitol Records, and now, has a thriving career as a singer/songwriter with numerous film and television placements.

"For me, there have been lots of little lightning strikes," says Trapper. Among those, he considers quitting his job to focus on music to be the first important one. Once The Push Stars formed, their first manager had a connection with filmmakers, the Farrely Brothers. That connection led to a song placement in the hit film *There's Something About Mary*.

The band's second manager had a connection with Rosemary Carroll, a well-connected entertainment attorney in New York. Carroll used her contacts to obtain a record deal for The Push Stars with Capitol Records. As he later realized, the time at Capitol really helped Chris in his solo career as well. "We got some great exposure from being on a major label, and I think a lot of my fans today are from The Push Stars," says the Boston-based singer.

One of the biggest breaks for The Push Stars was the opportunity to tour with Matchbox Twenty as the band's opening act for a U.S. Tour.

"Greg Collins engineered (The Push Stars record) *Paint The Town* and also did some work with Matchbox Twenty. He gave Rob Thomas a raw mix of the tracks. Rob liked the record a lot and asked us to come out on tour and open up for Matchbox Twenty. He watched all of our sets from the side of the stage. They really took a chance on us because it didn't meet any of the rules for an opening band for an arena tour. We weren't on a major label then. We didn't have a radio single. Somehow, we were able to do it and it was a great experience," remembers Trapper.

Trapper and The Push Stars recorded a very strong record with *Paint The Town*. It was so good that their engineer shared it with the front man of one of the most commercially successful mainstream rock bands of the last fifteen years. The Push Stars fan base grew because their music resonated with Rob Thomas. But, if another engineer had been used for Paint The Town, The Push Stars may have never had the Matchbox Twenty connection and certainly would not have opened up a U.S. Tour for Matchbox Twenty.

The Matchbox Twenty tour also led to more work for the band's drummer, Ryan MacMillan, who now plays drums for Matchbox Twenty.

QUICK TIPS

- Put yourself in position to make it more likely that good things will happen. You can do this by:
    - Playing live as much as possible
    - Being a part of a community of other artists
    - Being a likeable person
    - Finding the right professional support

- Try to use engineers, producers, and professional support personnel who have connections in the industry.

- As soon as your opportunity comes, capitalize on it by being ready to respond. Think about what would be the best-case scenario for you. Then, think about how you would handle it if it actually happened.

- Return emails.

CHAPTER 8

HOW TO GO FROM *WANTING* A CAREER AS AN ARTIST TO *HAVING* ONE

We have had the pleasure of interviewing some amazing, career-minded artists who provided thoughtful insight for this book. After all of those conversations, the best advice can be distilled with four major tips: (1) Be awesomely talented. (2) Be smart. (3) Be nice. (4) Be determined. (5) Be lucky.

1. Be Awesomely Talented.

While talent alone will not guarantee you a career as a musician, it certainly is important. There is a minimum threshold of talent that is necessary to have a real chance at being a professional musician. We like to think of this in terms of percentile scores, like on standardized tests or the presidential fitness test from elementary school. You don't need to be in the 99th percentile. You just need to pass the test, which is probably somewhere around the 80th percentile.

The less natural talent that you have, the more you need to work to sharpen your skills. Malcolm Gladwell says in his great book, *Outliers,* that people who are hyper-successful in anything typically spend about 10,000 hours practicing before they get to the peak of their prominence. So, like Gladwell says, practice makes really good. And we are talking about a crazy amount of practice – almost to the point where it consumes and defines you.

Some people are just born with natural talent. If you are truly amazing and can shock people, then your natural talent alone may be enough to get you where you need to be. That, however, is doubtful.

You know that guy you know who is better than the people you hear on the radio? You know, the guy whose songs you mix in with popular songs on playlists during parties? Assuming that he is unbelievable and truly is the cream of the crop, there are hundreds of other people just like him in America, and thousands more in the world. Chances are that no matter how good you are, someone is better, or at least as good.

Being awesomely talented helps. But it is only part of the equation. Talent is not a ticket to success. But lack of talent is a disqualifier from it. For that reason, it is important to first hone your craft, and then to focus on points two through five.

2. Be Smart.

The first key to success is pretty simple. Being smart is probably the most complex part of music career success. Being smart can be broken down in to three components: (1) professional support, (2) technology, and (3) defining your goal.

First, surround yourself with a good team. Bring people in at the appropriate time.

Managers are probably the first people to bring in on the ground level. Your manager needs to be someone who believes in what you are doing and is willing to truly go to bat for you as an artist. Be careful about signing with booking agents or trying to hire a lawyer before you really need one. When financial resources are scarce, a new amp may be more important than a legal consultation. (This is coming from an attorney!)

On the other hand, don't wait too long to bring the right people on to your team. Failing to have a lawyer review a document before you sign it can cause serious nightmares down the road. Read our interview with Johnny Lee for examples of professional relationship disasters.

Second, you need to use technology wisely. The bare minimum as of the printing of this book is to have a MySpace band page (I know that MySpace isn't as popular for social networking anymore, but trust me, it is still vital for bands.), a Facebook fan page, an iLike page, a Twitter account, and all of the other various social media. The trendy media will always be changing, and for new bands, it will always be important to have a grasp on what social media is being used by your target demographic to consume music.

Another technology tip is to collect information about your fans so that you can best serve them. Derek Webb, one of the founders of *NoiseTrade*, collected 80,000 zip codes of people who downloaded his music to discover that two of his biggest fan bases were in towns where he had never played: New York and Los Angeles.

Now, he plays In New York and L.A. every year and is consistently selling out bigger venues each time. Without the information about fans that he gained from giving away free downloads, he never would have played those shows. Being informed about your fans and keeping your fans informed about your career through mailing lists and social media will nurture the artist-fan relationship, which is a big piece of the puzzle in making a career as an artist.

The third, and probably the most important part of being smart is to have a clear definition of your short-term career goal. Once you determine your goal, you will be able to plan your next steps. This is where geography comes in to play.

If all that you care about is playing music and attracting fans who believe in your music, then your target audience is the fans – NOT the music industry. If you are trying to get fans, one of the most difficult places to be is Nashville, New York, or L.A. Go to an open mic in those cities and you will see what I mean. Most of the people on stage are unbelievably talented, and the people in the crowd are so used to it and jaded by the sheer number of super-talented people that no one cares. The best places to get fans are where there is less competition for fans.

Also, if your music is a niche that is not commercially marketable, you may be relegated to pursuing fans, even if you want to be a mega star. Don't expect a major label to sign your Right Wing polka jam band. It's not going to happen. Ultimately, pop music must be popular.

Conversely, if you don't have a following of fans yet *and* you believe that your talent is ready to go to the next level, the other option is to make the music industry and record label executives your audience.

After all of the interviews in this book, what we learned is that the people who get on the radio and get record deals are out there playing as many shows as they can and making as many friends as they can. And, *if the goal is to get signed by a major record label and have an A&R rep find them*, they are doing those things from Nashville, New York, or L.A., or they have very strong personal connections with the music industry in Nashville, New York, or L.A.

However, there is a terrible catch 22 with trying to appeal to the music industry gate keepers in the Music Cities. Those are the best (and probably the only) places to launch a career by getting signed to a record label. Everyone else who is trying to launch a career knows that. When you combine that with the recorded music industry being in a state of flux and confusion, it makes it really hard to be the one person who gets signed to a major label with no pre-existing fan base.

As Derek Webb says, moving to a major Music City and trying to make it as an artist is like being a needle and jumping into a haystack.

Because of that, we believe that the best way to pursue a career is to go the organic route and focus on fans, not the record labels. The problem with that bit of advice is that some people are still getting signed by moving to Music Cities and jumping into the haystack. Major labels have to sign someone. And, yes, it could be you.

Erin McCarley and Griffin House were both beneficiaries of this phenomenon. They were signed prior to developing a large fan base. They never would have been signed to the labels that they are currently on if they did not live in Nashville. That doesn't mean that they wouldn't have built an organic fan base on their own. They just didn't have to do it on their own because the label provided a platform that helped them to get started.

3. Be Nice.

Make friends. Don't network just so that you can ride someone's coattails. Make real friendships with people that you like to hang out with who also are musicians. Eventually, if you are around other people who have a genuine interest in pursuing music, some of your friends will have success. When those people have success, they are likely to help you out. A great example of this is Griffin House being shopped by major labels on the recommendation of his friend, Dave Barnes, who was helped by Marc Broussard.

If you happen to move to one of the major Music Cities, be humble, even if you are unbelievably talented. Just being a nice person who is not annoying and is tolerable to be around can give you a huge advantage in a music industry that is very relationship based and filled with prima donnas.

4. Be Determined.

Trying to sell your music to people for a living is difficult. The supply far outweighs the demand. There will always be people who say that you are not good enough. I've heard it said hundreds of times that Micheal Jordan was cut from his freshman high school basketball team. Can you imagine that? The musical equivalent of this would be an A&R rep hearing The Beatles and saying, "I just don't see it catching on in the States." (The Beatles were actually rejected by five different record labels before finally signing with EMI!)

The key for you, the aspiring artist, is that you can't let the negative comments or naysaying of anyone deter you from pursuing music. If you really want it, go after it with everything. The people who ultimately succeed are people who dive in and put all of their eggs in the music basket.

Sure, you may have to work other jobs to make ends meet. But, you will never hear of a brain surgeon who is trying to continue with brain surgery and have a career as a musician. That guy is a brain surgeon with a hobby of music. He is not a career minded musician. If you want music to be your career, you need to make sure that you treat it like a career and not a hobby.

People love to share their opinions, which is fine, except that most people don't know what they are talking about, especially when it comes to the music industry. The good news is that everyone doesn't have to like your music. You only need to have enough fans to sustain a career.

If music is going to be your business, treat it like one. You are a small business owner and the widgets you are selling are your songs, your performance, and yourself.

There is a great essay online called 1000 True Fans, which Derek Webb mentioned earlier in the book. The point of the essay is that you really only need 1000 people who love your music to be able to have a career in music.

For example, if you play three shows per year and charge $10 for tickets, and 1,000 fans go to the show, then you will have made $30,000 on live performances. If you also put out a record every year for $10, and those 1000 fans also bought the record, then you would be making another $10,000 in a year. The numbers keep going up with additional revenue sources and higher price points.

Whether or not you believe that the number of fans that you need is 1,000, isn't important. The point is that it doesn't take *that many* fans to have a thriving music career if the fans are dedicated to you and will actually support you financially.

You can "do music" as a career. This is the hardest time to be discovered by a major record label and get signed. It is the hardest time to be a huge rock star. However, it is possible to make a living as a musician by focusing on a few fans and then continuing to grow and develop your fan base.

5. Be Lucky.

It pains us to include a factor outside of anyone's control as a step to a career as an artist. However, this book is about real life. It is about how artists have actually had success and how you can do the same in your career. The reality is that a career in music is risky. You might do everything the right way and not have a career in music, or have a struggling career.

Gabe Dixon agrees. "Music is an unconventional career. I was just talking about this with Dave Barnes the other day about how much luck is involved with success in music. You can work fairly hard, be an amazing singer, songwriter and player, be a good-looking person, have a great team, and it can still not work out for you. It's just because of the nature of business and conditions and any number of factors. I think those are the things you have to rise through," says Dixon.

While luck will play a role in your career in some form, there is nothing that you can do about luck. On the other hand, as discussed throughout this book, you *can* do things to put yourself in a position to be more likely to be lucky. The role of luck in a music career should not be a shock. Just be aware that luck matters and focus on what you *can* do.

In most instances, where artists claim to have been "lucky," that luck was actually a relationship or connection that recognized the artist's talent at an opportune time. In that regard, a major facet of "being lucky" is making the right relationships and making those connections in a thoughtful way.

Saying that luck matters is just another way of saying that lightning has to actually strike. You've been given the tools to make it more likely for lightning to strike throughout this book. You have to be very talented. You have to be persistent. You have to have clarity around your goals. If you do all of these things and keep pursuing music, the chances that you will be "lucky" will significantly increase.

No matter what route you choose, we wish you the best, and hope to hear you in the future, whether on the radio or in a dive bar.

CHAPTER 9

PARTING ADVICE FROM ARTISTS

Before we concluded each interview, we asked the artists what they would tell someone who wants to have a career in music. Some of the answers were detailed. Some were very brief. Here is the combined advice of all of the artists we interviewed, directed specifically at you, the up and coming artist.

Johnny Lee

"I'd tell them the same thing Loretta Lynn told me the first time that she met me: write. You've got to write songs. Writing is like working out. The more you do it, the better you get at it.

And make sure that your ass is covered. Don't let a record company put you so far into debt that if you don't make them millions of dollars, they will shit can you. That will happen. Have some representation. Learn something about finances and where to put some money, if you are lucky enough to make some, so you can take care of yourself later on. Because one day, they will shit can you. It will happen one day. Look at Alabama. They had a great run. But, it ain't happening no more. No matter how good you are. You will get shit canned. So, cover your ass."

Marti Dodson (Saving Jane)

"I would tell them that the hardest thing to take is constant rejection and constant criticism.

You really have to believe in yourself. If you don't, you will never make it. And you have to be tough. We shopped *Girl Next Door* to Universal five times. And five times they said, 'No, we don't think this is anything.' Then, it went on the radio [through another label] and they said, 'About that record. . .' So, you have to believe in your music and in what you are doing and remember that everybody has been turned down. Madonna got turned down. Aerosmith got turned down. Somebody thought they were nobody at some point."

Jerry DePizzo (O.A.R.)

"It depends on the situation that you are in. If you are in a band like O.A.R. and people are coming to the shows, keep doing it on your own for as long as you can, until a great or lucrative opportunity comes your way. What helped O.A.R. the most is that we were able to do so much legwork on our own that the labels could come in and take us to the next level.

Do as much as you can on your own. Educate yourself. When you are going to sign, bring other people in, make sure that there are like-minded individuals who share the same goals and values as you do and you feel comfortable with them."

Griffin House

"Go for it! That's all I would say. Just go for it. Live out of your heart and try not to think too much. Just do it."

Five Times August

"I would probably say not to give up. I have done a lot of cool things. But there are days when you really want to give up. It takes its toll on you driving across the country. Sleeping in vans, eating three-dollar happy meals for breakfast, lunch, and dinner.

I've had a lot of opportunities. There have been some that seemed like the easier way, but I didn't take them because they didn't feel right. There were opportunities that would have invaded on my morals and values that would have gotten me more press. I've never done anything that I didn't approve of or that I was ashamed of."

Erin McCarley

"Part of me wants to say forget college and dive into the creative thing. Get a part time job in a city where there is a really tight community of musicians, where it is supportive and positive. Part of me says to do that.

But, as a senior in college, I was not ready emotionally to deal with the songs that needed to be written, or just the business in general. So, each step is important. You have to have patience, or else you are going to burn out really fast. I think I am an encouragement to people because I am thirty years old and I just started writing songs five years ago.

Some of the best advice I got was 'Don't be in a hurry to get out on the road and haphazardly go for it.' Sit down. Make a plan. Write some songs that, when you go out on stage, you feel 100% perfect with playing every night, because you are going to be playing them every night if you end up having a career as an artist. It is a little more grueling doing that process, but I wouldn't take back the time that was allotted for that. And, just the process of being able to figure out who I was."

Derek Webb

"Take advantage of all of the things that the Internet affords. Don't manufacture unless you have to. Keep it digital. Spend as little money as you can. Approach it like you are starting a small business. That's really what you are doing. It's blue-collar work. It is not fame and fortune. And, if it is fame and fortune, it is not like you think it is. Ask the people who have it. Trust me.

A career in music is a real job. You have to work really hard at it. It is like any small business, where you will have a few years where you won't make any profit. You have to be ready for that. Go into some debt if you have to. It is work that you will really enjoy as long as your expectations are set right. Playing music is a real job and you can do it. It just requires that your expectations are gauged correctly.

I'd recommend getting into Seth Godin and reading *Tribes*. There is an essay online called 1000 True Fans that lays the economy out of why you really only need about a thousand people who are super-devoted to what you are doing and support you to make a living. As long as you can be satisfied with that, that is really all it takes. What that means is making good connections, harvesting information, really working hard to know who those fans are and make impressions with them, and to not look over those people's heads for your future fans. Look all those people in the face. Confess to the fact that you all need each other. They need your art in their lives and you need them to sustain you.

Don't go the other way of disappearing into the mystique of the limo when the show is over. Pour yourself into those people. In Caedmon's, we used to tell people in every college town where we played, 'We are going to IHOP after the show.' Everybody come. It would be Caedmon's Call, party of 65. We would bounce around from table to table. By our second year, we knew two-thirds of the people at every show. I still know a lot of those people. As I travel the country, I hang out with them. I call them on my way into town and have meals with them and their families as we have all gotten older.

That's what it is all about. It is relational. Don't kid yourself and say that it is not. It is blue-collar work. You need those people as much as they need you. The more you can embrace that, the easier time you are going to have."

Chris Trapper

"Don't put the commerce before the art. The art has to go before the commerce. Listening back to some of The Push Stars records, sometimes I feel like they were reactionary because we needed some money at the time. You have to focus on your craft. The commerce will come if the art is good enough.

The other thing is that you have to surround yourself with people who are supportive of what you are doing. Don't date a girl who is a doubter and doesn't believe in what you are doing."

Dave Barnes

"I would warn that [a music career] is not what you think it is. Hey, kid who watched MTV who sees Rob Thomas playing and there's hot girls in the video. Hey, girl who thinks Taylor Swift is awesome. That is true, what they are doing looks cool and fun. But, the sacrifices that people make to do this, especially at that level, you have no way to comprehend.

So, the only thing that can soothe that beast is the obsession – you have to power through. I have to do this. You have to think about it all the time. That's the beginning of it, if you are thinking about music all the time. That's not the fruition. If you think its fun and you enjoy playing your guitar every now and then, I don't think this is for you.

There isn't a path. And if you can accept that, and you can keep that passion for it burning, you will find something."

Joe Pisapia (Guster)

"It's worth a shot, if it's your passion, if it's what you love, you're constantly going to be redefined, as far as your drive. If it's your passion, you deserve to yourself to try it, to see what happens because you may not ever be secure, but security is being redefined right now anyway.

You have to go for it, and you have to have patience to create a life and a career with a meaning and a purpose. And as much as you have to stick to your guns, in terms of your personality and your passions, you also have to create sense of flexibility, because who knows where this stuff is going to come from. Keep it open about how you're going to get there."

Gabe Dixon

"I would say when it comes to having a career in music, don't do it for the money because that's not a reason to do anything. With music you can't count on it to necessarily pay your bills. You have to do it for the love. And I feel if you truly love it and you're truly putting all your heart and soul into it, then you're going to have a career in it somehow. Even if it's not exactly what you set out or what you thought you were going to be doing.

I just say it's got to start with love. It's got to start with a love of music and if you don't have that and you're just thinking, 'Oh, I'm going to be a rock star,' that stuff is fleeting. But having a career in music is a completely different thing than being a rock star.

If you make money, spend your money wisely. Don't spend everything you make, because like with anything, with any self-employed person, when you're in music, you're the head of your corporation. You're in charge. And I think a lot of people don't really realize that.

A music career is very entrepreneurial in nature. It's similar to a lot of people who start their own business because if you're a musician you have a product that no one else has. They may have the same type of product, but Crest is not Colgate. You have something unique to market to the world. You have to realize it's up to you ultimately to market it.

Also, there are ways that you can have a career in the music by jumping on other people's careers. You can play for other people or you can work in the music industry somewhere, but ultimately you have your own trajectory.

Oh, and marry someone who has a career outside of music."

INTERVIEWS

Dave Barnes

TK: Music is a lot different from other career paths, right?

DB: Yes. I do think the negative of a job that is- the hard thing is how do you prove you're a better accountant than somebody else? And that's the beauty of music. You can, though it is subjective, you know how a certain song makes you feel compared to another one. Like when I listen to "Jump" by Van Halen compared to some song of that same time that was doing the same thing. "Jump"' is going to affect me more you know, where as if you're an accountant and you got an "A" on your exam and the other guy got an "A" well then who wins? Then it's a personality thing, so you get into a lot more things, it's not as cut and dry, that's for sure. There is some sense you get to have faith in a process a little more than you do as a musician. You don't get to rest on "well this pretty much works a lot of the time". You go to this college, you get this degree, you work there, and hey you're an accountant. So it's a little more of a toss up [with music].

TK: I agree.

DB: It's hard for me to watch people – 2 different types of people. One, People who are extremely talented that should be known better that aren't who are scraping, trying to get by in careers but they *are* talented. You could put them with anybody in any town and say, "do you think this person's talented?" and they would say "immensely talented." Now, why they're not known, why it's not working who knows, right?

Compared to the guy or girl who's really not that talented but is just getting after it, getting after it, getting after it, going and going. The frustration of having people that can't make it should and the people that are trying so hard and shouldn't. It's not the same, but it's the same fervor of like- it's just hard to watch. It's hard to watch the people you hear about that should be killing it but aren't and it's hard to watch people that you're like "no offense, but this isn't that great. Have you thought about doing something else?" It's that same fire in me that can get sort of overwhelmed feeling like, and I'm not God, I don't know if someone's going to make it or not, but there's some sense of like "hey I don't know that the gift set you have is worth banking on like you are", you know. And it's just hard, it can get really hard. Especially in Nashville where there's so much of both. There's so many people that should be huge and there's so many people that shouldn't be doing it in some ways.

TK: Ok, well do you have any Dave Barnes thesis statement; do you have any closing remarks here?

DB: Not without crying, I'll just tear up. Thank you so much. I don't think so. I mean, I love these interviews because it always makes me laugh to myself. Doing 'We'd love to hear how you got where you were,' well, this is going to be the most boring interview of all time, because it's not a story of what I've done as much as the doors that have been opened for me.

TK: Well man I've got to say this, I'm interviewing all these different people in all these different arenas and different levels of success and I love it that I've finally found some consistency in a world that – like we're all together in this. It's weird that, almost more than anything, doing this has kind of made me believe that again. I kind of lost sight of that, I think I had started to feel a little frustrated and resentful and feeling like I was missing the point.

DB: I don't know anybody – I mean look at Gabe's story. The guy worked with Eddie Kramer and then he worked with Paul McCartney. That wasn't something where Gabe was knocking down doors, he was just playing his music.

TK: Tell me about your touring strategy.

DB: You know what, I will say this, because I think this will help, because I didn't speak to this much. But when you talk about a concentric thing, that's one of the few things I really did decide when I started playing music. I looked at it this way, I could either go out – let's say this was like 2 years into my career – I could either go out and play a ton of shows to a few people or I can build a buzz in markets and play them twice a year to 200 or 300 people each time. And that *really* worked for me. Because instead, I saw some people around me who were like 'we're just going to go play, we'll play anywhere and whatever' and I thought 'you know what I'm going to do, I'm going to bank on buzz.'

If people know I only play a market twice a year, they're probably more apt to come out than if I play four times. Because I just thought, 'I don't want to do that, I didn't want to spend my time building markets that far away that are going to be really cost heavy,' and so I think that model served me really well.

I mean, when I hired my manager one of the first things I said was, 'Chris, I'm not the guy who's going to go out and play a million dates a year.' Really, more because I don't think for what I do it's smart. I'd rather play two big shows a year in markets and really see people come to those than to play four times and over four shows have as many as I did for two.

But so that sort of concentric thing I did, a band like O.A.R. did the same thing, but they did it to a huge degree. I did it on a much smaller degree, like I'm sort of going to bank on buzz and not an inaccessibility oddly enough in a touring scenario helping me and then by the time I'm really starting to draw them out I'll play a regular – like a pretty regular pace.

But yeah, that stuff is fascinating to me. How people sort of put that together. And I think that's something a lot of artists don't get is you've got to get people wanting, especially today. I think if you're new, the last thing you want is overload.

If you're new you actually want to be a little hard to get. Because you'll be the 1 out of 50 that's like "why's that dude, he doesn't have any videos up. I'm dying to know more about him. Oh my God he posted a video, uh it's 20 seconds long, come on dude" as opposed to "here's my house I grew up in, here's my mom, here's my sister, here's the girl I'm dating right now, here's my new guitar" you know. It's like I don't like you enough to want to know that. Make me want to like you and then once I like you I'll want to know that.

TK: How do you decide when that is as an artist?

DB: Who knows, man, who knows?

TK: Okay.

DB: I think you'll know. I think you're kind of like alright the buzz is building there's some people who I'm getting frequent emails now being like "dude when are you posting your video" or like "you haven't updated your bio."

TK: Have you always been, I just realized this is something I meant to ask you, were you always really keyed in to what your fans were thinking? Did you try to communicate with them or keep up with that sort of dialogue?

DB: Yeah. You know my thing is I'm such a fan of other bands that I've always listened to my gut and it's served me pretty well. I've been off before, but I'm a fan and that's the best thing and the worst thing about me is that I love music. I love bands. I love artists, I love CD packages. I love the CD art. I'm just a fan.

And so I look at what I want and go, "Okay, so and so hasn't put up a video in awhile, I'd probably like that. So how long has it been? 6 months? That's too long. Let's do 3 months. Then, I'll put up a video in 3 months" or "You know what I like about that guy? I love that he is funny. I love it when I get his twitter posts. He's really humorous. I want to be more humorous."

I'm privileged. I'm just a huge music fan. My test audience is sort of myself. I sort of think like "God that guy is putting out an EP and he released a record a year ago what does that say to me, that makes me think that maybe he's quaking or man this scares me a little bit so is that CD going to be good? I don't want to do that. Or this is cool he put out a seasonal thing.

I do that a lot with myself. I tend to be really like, I'll watch myself with the way that I react to things. It's a pretty scary bet because I don't think a lot of people like me. But so far it's done me pretty well. From who I tour with to- I'm hyper sensitive to perception and so- which sucks, but it serves me pretty well you know. I would see bands I really respected when they go on tour and was like, "Why would you do that tour?" and whether I liked it or not would kind of affect how I viewed them. I'd be like "God, I wouldn't think they would do that tour."

TK: Counting Crows did that. They were doing all these – they did Sheryl Crow, they did John Mayer. It made sense. It kept them more vital. I've always been a fan of the band and then they did this one tour, I don't remember, maybe two years ago with Collective Soul and Live or something. I was like are you going to be touring County fairs next? I felt like they were packaging themselves as such a, it's 1996 and we're watching *Friends.* It was like a Generation X, visit the past type thing. It was really weird; I just thought it was a terrible decision. But I don't know.

DB: That's exactly it. That's that same thing I listen to in my head. You know, Chris will send me thoughts "what if we do something like this?" I'll be like "you know man, I don't think so, because I really think I would really perceive that this way" or "we should do that because I don't want to be perceived that way" you know, whatever the decision is.

Like I said, it's done me well up till now. As I get older I realize I'm a pretty quirky music fan. So things that I like, I don't know that the new generation cares about. And that's something I've been proved wrong a few times. I can't think of anything specific, but there's times I've been like "no that wouldn't work and I was like wow that really worked. I was wrong." Because there's new avenues I haven't known about before that I think are weird, but people think they are completely normal. You know, I think one [avenue] is the output of music. The EP, I was kind of like "I don't know if this is too soon to put out an EP less than a year after I put a record out" and the EP did really well, so I was like, "Ok, well wrong about that one". So I think there's a pace that I'm not familiar with to today's listener that I'm still learning. They have a pretty veracious appetite.

TK: I think so. I also think that it's fighting with something about the attention span thing. You kind of do have to be in front of people all the time. Like, "Hey look over here, don't forget about me. I know that there's new guys. I know there's a new TV show, but I'm still here." I guess that is the benefit of having all these different pieces of media you can put out. More music or free downloads or a video, whatever. There are a lot of ways to stay in front of people, to remind people you're still doing stuff.

DB: I think it is a vital thing man. Just for today, it might not be in 5 years or 10 years but, today it's huge that people know that you're still around. That it's not, "God where did Fleetwood Mac go for 3 years before they put out this record." Back then it was like "Wow, I don't know, we can't ever know that, but man it's out and we're going to go buy it." Today it's like "is he still doing music? He hasn't tweeted in a month, is he alive?" you know.

Gabe Dixon

TK: Tell me about getting signed to a major label.

GD: I feel like we got pretty lucky. But, the thing that – I don't know if fickle is the word – the thing that is f'ed up about big labels, and the biggest lesson we learned, is that you can't count on them to make it happen for you. They're not going to develop your base. Because they don't know if the guy that signed you is going to be there the next day, you know.

So that's what happened to us. We got signed by a guy that produced a record for us. It was great. And then a new president came in and he was gone. So he was gone and we didn't have anybody at the label that really gave a shit about us. But we were out on tour, touring the whole country as if we have had some kind of radio single or something, which we didn't. And we kind of abandoned our base a little bit, you know.

So I think one of the things that I feel important for a band is to nurture your base and nurture your base of support. Because that's the only thing that's truly real. If you have a hit on the radio, in my mind, if you have a hit on the radio but you can't go and play to a big room full of people anywhere, then, enjoy it while it lasts because it's not going to last very long.

I think a great thing about what's happening with music right now is everything's becoming a lot more real as far as what success is and people are less dependent upon these giant major label behemoths. But the cool thing about the Warner Brothers deal was that it did get us in the studio, we got to make a really expensive record and we got to tour for a year and a half, meet a lot of great people from bands like Guster, O.A.R., Littlefeet, all these great bands, Norah Jones. And we got to see how other people did things and I think that's helped us to keep this going for a long time.

TK: How has being a classically trained musician helped you in your career?

GD: I think one of the reasons I'm thankful I went to college is that I did get to focus a lot on making myself better, not only as a singer and as a songwriter but as a piano player. I was a piano major. Even though I don't play classical music very much at all anymore, for about four years there I was playing it nearly every day for like three hours. That alone just got my piano chops up so much that it enables me to go and play with people who will pay me to play for them. It enabled me to play with Paul McCartney on his record and that was kind of in the midst of all the things happening for my band with Warner Brothers.

That was kind of like the icing on the cake in that situation. It also has enabled me to – and through that I've sort of gotten the attention of other people like Alison Kraus, and ultimately Loggins & Messina, people like that. I go in and I can really do a good job playing on their stuff, you know. And singing background vocals and so- In times where my thing with my band has not been doing anything like after our Warner's deal kind of fizzled out. I was able to sustain myself at least in part through playing music with other people.

If I were just a songwriter maybe I could have gotten a publishing deal or if I was just a singer I might be able to sing some jingles or some this or that but I think having that – being able to play the piano allowed me to do that and sing on peoples things and write songs and so I had this diversification of sort of income that's really been my saving grace, you know. Because it didn't happen with Warner Brother's.

TK: What happened in that initial transition period? Are there any mistakes maybe that you felt you made and how did you correct that? What did you do moving forward to kind of get you to where you are now?

GD: Ultimately, when we lost our Warner Brother's deal we were all kind of living in separate cities because I had moved all my stuff back to Nashville and so, eventually we decided to get the band together and so all three of us went back to Nashville, or went to Nashville and started playing in one place again. And I think it's because we did that and continued our career again on our own terms that we went on to get another record deal and to put out another record last year and do something that we're really interested in.

The thing I love to do the most is sing and play my own songs for other people. That's not something I can count on making me a living all the time even though at the moment it is. I know that I need to still be able to play with other people and write songs with other people that maybe other people cut and that kind of thing. The more skills you have the better I guess.

TK: Okay, and who are you with now label wise?

GD: It's called Concord music group, Fantasy records.

TK: After the initial kind of experience you had in New York and with Warner Brother's, how did you get to where you are now?

GD: Our producer who produced our Warner Brother's record, David Kahn, he was producing Paul McCartney's record the next month and so I went in a did an organ pass on one of our songs and he said "man" and I came back in he was like "that was really good, do you want to play on Paul's record?" I was like "I think I'm going to go puke and I'll be right back."

TK: I feel like the diversification thing is kind of continued here. How did you get to this point where you're at now?

GD: Well, first of all it wasn't without day jobs for awhile there, you know. I was definitely working my share of valet stuff, things like that for a little while after the Warner Brother's experience. I guess what happened was after I moved my stuff from New York to Nashville my girlfriend at the time, who is now my wife, she moved to Ashville, NC. So I sort of started spending a lot of time in Ashville, just writing songs and I wrote a song called "All will be well" that ended up on an EP.

Our manager got us a deal with WXPN radio station in Philadelphia. They had a venue called World Café Live and a radio show called World Café. We hadn't even at that time all lived in Nashville. We did like one rehearsal and we hadn't played in months and we went up and played these new songs at World Café.

But even before we recorded the World Café thing, I had been writing. I just wrote, and wrote and wrote and we just recorded, and recorded, and recorded and didn't really stop doing that even though we weren't making any money with this band at all for at least, 2003, 2004, and part of 2005. We had jobs and we just got together when we could and just kind of burned the candle at both ends trying to make this music get out there.

We recorded the World Café EP in Philadelphia in February of 2005 and I went back and was like "Ok, what's going to happen with it? We don't know." Somebody at Warner Brother's might help us out and put it out. We really weren't sure.

I went back to valet parking cars, you know, building up credit card debt, stuff like that. Fun stuff. And then I got the call from Loggins and Messina in March. They said "Hey, we'll pay you a good amount of money to come out on tour with us." So I went and did that for that summer, that sustained me and helped me financially and gave me another excuse to be playing all the time, which is always good. Even for my own thing, just sparks new ideas and gets me going. And then 2005 the EP came out. Did a little tour on it for like a month and it was kind of cool. There were some people there somehow at the shows. I don't know how they heard about it but they did.

Nothing really happened for a little while after that. And then in February 2006, somebody at NBC who was the music supervisor for a show called *Conviction*, it's not even on the air anymore, got the EP from our manager a couple months before. And loved the song "All Will Be Well" so much that he put it in all the trailers for the show *Conviction*, which is like a Law & Order show. So it played all throughout the Olympics that year and just all these opportunities started opening up for us all of a sudden.

Then, that same song got into another show that Fall called *What About Brian*. Things started to build a little bit, we still weren't making a living necessarily, but money was starting to come in a little bit and we had all moved to Nashville at that point. We started playing around Nashville. Third & Lindsley and smaller places. And started to actually get something happening here to where we say we're going to play and people actually show up in large numbers to see us play. So that was pretty exciting.

And then somehow, there was a convergence at this label called Concord of people who my manager had worked with in the past or he knew of that were really good that had come from other labels. He thought they had really assembled a good team over there so we did a couple showcases, thought about signing with a different label and blah blah blah ended up signing with Concord Records.

They gave us some money to do a record and we decided we wanted to do it in Nashville, because like that was our thing. So we recorded at Blackbird and got a nice placement last year in this show called One Tree Hill for a song that's on the record and people started working for us all of a sudden. We had a whole team at the label. It was like our management grew, you know what I mean. From there, the record has started subtly selling more and more. And we got to be on the Craig Ferguson show and Jimmy Kimmel in January and so things started just moving along for us.

The other thing about early on, we not only had a good manager but I did develop a friendship with a really good lawyer who helped us work through some of the early- like our first independent record we did down in Miami with Eddie Kramer. He helped us work through that kind of contract and things like that.

TK: A lot of what you have said confirms a lot of what I learned just going through the music industry myself. Do you have a positive spin to put on it?

GD: Yes. Well, I get to play music for a living. My work day is different every day. Which for me, I have to have. I'm not someone who can go to the same job every single day. That drives me insane. You know, one day I'm at home playing the piano, practicing, writing. The next day, I'm doing a recording session with somebody I respect and the next day I'm answering all my fan Facebook emails and writing a blog and managing all the emails and shit that I have. I mean that's cool with me. I think that you have to be able to be okay with uncertainty and with instability for awhile in order to get to a place where you do have stability. But when I'm on stage playing for people and they really appreciate it, that just makes it all worth it.

TK: If you could give a sound bite of advice for aspiring musicians, what would it be?

GD: I would say, "get out there and play for people". Get something together and – book a gig first of all for yourselves. And you know practice it and go out there and show what you've got. Don't be afraid to do that as often as possible, because that's the way people are going to know what it is that you do. What it is that you want to do? And find allies that like your music and want to help you out. And don't be afraid of other artists and like share what you do with them and play music with other people and if somebody else who is your peer is having success that's a good thing, that's not a bad thing. Because it's all connected. Get out there and do your thing.

Joe Pisapia (Guster)

TK: Do you think a college education helped you in your career?

JP: For me, college was about almost having a 4 year vacation of forging good relationships. I wasn't really into the academic part of it. Sure, I learned stuff. But, I was too immature to get into studies at that point. Had I known, had I had real clarity over like, I'm really going to go for this, I probably could have saved money and not gone. But it was just more of a societal thing, you go to college when you finish high school you know.

TK: Do you have anything to share about the period of time between when you decided you wanted a career in music to the time you actually started to have one?

JP: It's funny because I have friends who are younger than I am and they're in their mid to late 20's and they're getting antsy with all this stuff. But this is the time period where everything gets forged. The period where you're really starting to get antsy but there's so much potential. And when you're that young you don't really need any money. You can sleep on a mattress. You're portable. It's the best age because you don't need anything. My advice is to ride that out as long as you can. Try not to get into this comfort zone thing. Keep it simple.

But I remember years ago thinking that one day I'll make my living through music. Then, I stopped and realized that the last two years I had already been making my living doing music. I'm not making a killing but that's what I do. I was like, 'That's pretty sweet.' That was sort of one of those little 'ah ha' moments that you have.

But I had to hit the total rock bottom before things started to turn around. I had one summer when I was traveling doing some solo shows in the Northeast, and my van broke down coming back from Vermont. I was stranded for two months in Pennsylvania and I had nowhere to turn. I had to borrow money from my mom. I was already 32. So, I thought this career in music is not going to happen. I had to figure something out. Eventually, all of that turned around.

TK: Did you have a manager at any point in time before you had any financial success or did that come afterwards?

JP: It all came after. I mean early on in Joe, Marc's Brother stuff we had a producer who helped us in a lot of managerial ways and there were other people that helped us. But we never stuck around with them because nothing ever really got off the ground. Then we realized that you have to create it yourself and then get a manager involved because they can't do it for you. It's no fault of anybody's. I think that the business, or success or whatever comes from what the band is doing. The manager just keeps it organized once it's been formed.

TK: Is being in Nashville really key for you as far as being in a network, in a community where you can find a lot of work?

JP: Originally when we came to Nashville, sixteen years ago, it was hard to break in to. There wasn't as much indie stuff going on back then. It was more you were either in the system or you were out. It was really hard to become a niche person. We weren't really concerned with it though, we were concerned with the fact it was so cheap to live there and you could do awesome stuff. We would just practice all the time and play and write music and whatever. And that was great for us because we figured out that we worked three days a week at restaurants and have four days to rehearse and practice and it was like you don't get to do that in many towns. I would think now a days it's a lot harder to do that with the cost of living going up. But back then it was a sweet deal.

But I don't know if it was key. Nashville's a very difficult town. I know so many people in Nashville who I think are really awesome but the rest of the world doesn't know about them. I think it can be a little harder there for certain people. I love it because I feel like it's really community based.

I would think other towns would have a different feeling, like L.A. for instance. The feeling out there is way higher than Nashville. People find a different level of success, financial success because of the whole film thing. Its' like Nashville you're at the $5 black jack table and L.A. you're at the Bacharach table for $100 minimum with the film industry. I don't mean to be negative about it. I like it for different reasons. I define success differently too.

TK: So for aspiring musicians or aspiring musical career people do you- what is your personal opinion about the major music areas, New York, Nashville, L.A. versus anywhere else in the country?

JP: If you're in a band, it's better to be from the middle of nowhere. Sometimes it's better to be from Wichita, Kansas because then you create a story. Like for instance, My Morning Jacket, from Louisville, Kentucky. That created a story. If they had been from Nashville, Tennessee, people might have been suspicious of the fact that they were crafted or engineered with the intent of marketeting this thing rather than being pure.

TK: Briefly going back to your initial part of your career. How do you feel about what you did right and what were your mistakes in terms of connecting with fans, making industry connections, things like that?

JP: In the past one of the mistakes that we made was that we just weren't able to tour enough. That's one of the things I loved about Guster before I started playing with them. They toured so much early on in their career. When you're twenty something years old you get in a van and you can rough it, sleep in the van, go everywhere, be everywhere at all times and create those fan bases. And now that's what they own.

How many people are buying records? Not a lot. But if you have a touring base then you can make a living. You may not be able to make it on selling recordings. So, I wish we could have toured more.

As far as what I did right, I just think sticking to your guns about your style, your tastes. I think that's a good thing. For instance, I like all kinds of music. I'm not afraid to put country elements into a production or dance elements or whatever. I like music for what it is. And I don't want to be pigeonholed into one thing or the other and I think that because of the fact that if you really have a style or desire to say something to do something, it might take you longer to make a living at it. But I don't know if there's any other way to get around it.

TK: Tell me about your relationship with Guster and how that came about.

JP: Actually, back when I was doing my solo record those guys were writing the songs for *Keep it Together*. Ryan had come over to my place when they were playing in Nashville and we ended up writing a song for *Keep it Together* called 'Jesus on the Radio.' It was kind of what I was into on my record. It was folksy and loud and was a song you would be able to sing around the campfire.

So, we wrote the song around that time and they ended up recording it. I went up and recorded it with them at Woodstock. Then, we just became friends. We were kind of becoming friends before that, but then we just became better friends. When *Keep It Together* got done they had put too many overdubs on it that they said 'hey, we're going to have a hard time performing this record' because it was kind of unlike their prior stuff. They kind of flushed it out and said 'Would you come on the road with us for 3 or 4 months.' I said, 'Sure. That sounds like fun.'

At the time it sounded like a vacation. All I have to do is show up at 4 o'clock for sound check and 8 o'clock for the gig. I thought it was just going to be easy and fun. I did that, and of course, after awhile the fun wears off and becomes anything else.

And then it kind of turned out six years later, we started playing all their old songs and they were like 'What if we added banjo to this?' or 'What if we put keyboards on this?' Then we started rearranging everything and it became- and then we started writing for *Ganging up on the Sun*. They asked me to produce that one. So it was like we were becoming a band but they still respected me as someone outside to produce it. But it was really getting blurred as far as if I was in the band or wasn't. As we wrote together the intimacy got closer and I was in the band at that point, even though I was producing it with them.

I always admired those guys because of their work ethic and how hard they stayed out on the road and did all that stuff. They have the touring thing down to a science. And now, of course, it's a whole new regime because everybody except for me in the band has babies. But they're really smart about trying to figure out how to keep things in balance.

TK: What would you like to convey as the moral of your story career wise?

JP: Even where we are right now in our economy, it's a weird thing because so many people have work in these occupations that they don't enjoy, but because of the security, they kept working there. When you work your whole life for retirement, it just seems counterproductive to living in the now.

In order to take on a career in music you might fall on your ass. But look how many people are falling on their ass right now who have worked at companies they didn't even enjoy. So I would say it's worth a shot if it's your passion, if it's what you love.

You're constantly going to be redefined, as far as your ego. Saying 'I'm going to prove I'm the shit' is only going to get you so far. Then that's going to wear off because it's just not going to fuel you anymore. Something else has to kick in.

If it truly is your passion, then you owe it to yourself to chase it, to just try it and see what happens. You may not ever be secure, but what is security? I think it's being redefined right now.

I would say you have to go for it and you have to have patience. Musicians you can always find a mindless job in a restaurant or something that doesn't take any energy from your spirit and then put it all into your music. It's worth a try.

I remember talking to my dad when I was 18 saying I want to do this. I remember what my dad said. He was like 'Well, I think you should do it.' I was surprised that he let me off so easy. He was like 'Well, it's not like you're 33 coming to me with this." Then, flash forward to 33 and it was kind of funny because I gave it a good twelve years and still didn't have anything happen. But then it started to kick in. But not in the way I thought it would.

That's the other thing I would have to say. You also have to create a sense of flexibility about where the career is going to come from. You don't know the details of the path. Hopefully they're going to guide you to where you're going to be eventually.

Five Times August

Matt: Talk a little bit about your first big break with MTV.

Brad: I remember getting this email that said "MTV music supervisor" in the subject line and reading it and thinking 'Holy Crap!' I was like 'Who is this guy?' All that it said is "Interested in getting your music on a MTV show? Can I get a free copy of a cd?" I was like, this guy either just wants a free copy of a CD, or it could be legit. If anything, I would lose a buck and a half on a CD.

So I sent it to him, and he used one song of the EP that I was telling you about. He used a song called better with you on the first season of Laguna Beach. It was 90 seconds out of a 30 minute episode, which is a long time. It was a montage, that was pretty much a music video for the song. My first placement was 90 seconds. At the end of the episode it said 'You just heard Five Times August."

At the end of the next week, my iTunes sales went up. My MySpace listens skyrocketed. I was like, “Awesome.”

Matt: Did you have a day job at this time?

Brad: Kind of. I met Kelly working in radio in Dallas. Her and this other guy were kind of managing me for awhile. They wrote in hours for me, but I didn’t really work there. After a while they found out what I wanted to do and what I was interested in doing, so they helped me.

Matt: Were there follow up conversations after you sent the first CD?

Brad: I overnighted the CD, and he had a license agreement for me for that song. It was on a few weeks later. We were all watching it. I had no idea how long the placement was going to be. I just knew they were using it. We had a watching party. It was great!

We decided to take a few songs off that EP and redo them and finish a full album. Once we did that, I sent him a few songs off the full record. He placed 4 of those on the next season of Laguna Beach. He pretty much signed a blanket license for the whole album. That was the next step for placements.

A lot of those music supervisors are in the same circles. Because a lot of other MTV shows started using my stuff after that. We started getting calls from other people and we really milked the MTV thing as soon as it happened. We started plastering that MTV logo everywhere: "Five Times August as heard on MTV's Laguna Beach, the Hills, whatever."

Tris: What was your market at that time? You were still in Texas, right?

Brad: In late 2005, we went for the first time to Oklahoma and other parts of Texas. Then, in April of 2006, we really went with a national tour. Kelly does all of the booking.

Matt: What was your approach to your first national tour?

Brad: It was a gradual build up. We figured out where our best markets were based on online sales. Our first run was three shows.

Kelly: We decided to do it because of the placements. MTV ended up using every song on that album many times. The nationwide fan base was growing. From that, we scheduled a mini tour of three dates in Chicago, Maryland, and Pennsylvania. We did that and came back home, just to see how it would go. Then, we scheduled a few more tours that were spuratic. There were 50 people at one show, couple hundred at one, and at Common Ground in Chicago, we sold out the day that we posted the show.

Brad: A lot of people do their first tour, and play for 2 or 3 people. Lose a lot of money. Then, they come back and play for 4 or 5 people. Its that gradual long ten year build that people used to have to do before the internet.

Tris: What did you do to connect all the dots together and capitalize?

Brad: I made a huge effort to talk to fans who wrote me and really connect with them. Being accessible to people. Spending 5 or 6 hours a day responding to messages. Making sure that everyone who wrote me got a response. Fans love it when you respond. I love doing that.

I remember going to see Guster. They were one of my favorite bands. I would drive to Austin to go see them and make that extra effort to stay around after the show and meet them and get autographs. I did it with Ben Folds and John Mayer. I've always looked at fans of my music in the same way that I was fans of other people's music.

Matt: You are unsigned and completely independent. Your career has been more successful than many signed artists on major labels. Do you intentionally stay independent as a business choice or as an artistic choice?

Brad: It has never been out of the question. When I started out, it was like, I've got to get a record label. That is the ideal situation for most new artists. That is the dream. I'm gonna get a record label. I'm gonna make a lot of money. I'm gonna be on tv. Probably about five years in to doing it myself, and after all the placements and talking with seven major labels, I just got this vibe, like I don't think they know what they are doing or what they want.

I looked at my career and thought, I've done a lot on my own. We have worked so hard. It would be such a risk to hand that over. There are some days where I am like, just sign. But, now it is at a point where I probably won't sign. The more the industry keeps changing, the less important record labels are. The more people that we have talked to that have gone that route, the more we realize that maybe we shouldn't.

Me and the record labels crossed paths. I wanted it bad when I started out and they didn't want me. Then, they kind of wanted me and I sort of wanted them, but I didn't sign. Now, they want me, but I don't want them.

Kelly: I was talking to the VP of one of the biggest labels. He wanted to do the Schmooze thing and come and meet with us. We had already met with Atlantic and Warner and Columbia. I was like, I will talk to Brad and see if he wants to. But, it is a risk for us. He said, "No one has ever said that signing to a label is a risk for us. You are telling me that if we make you an offer, you might not want it." And, I said, 'Yes. We are already making a living at this. It is different for us.' If you take 85% of what we are making away, we can't live on 15%.

Brad: There is a level of comfort too. I have constantly built my career and it is constantly going up. I could sign to a label and be the next big think for 10 minutes. But, I would rather constantly build my career. And just be around for awhile, with people always talking about me. Rather than being old news.

Matt: How important is fan interaction to building a sustainable career?

Brad: Right now it is important. It wasn't as big before because there were so many stars that no one could reach. That's why people used to scream at the Beatles. You don't really get that now, except for the Jonas Brothers, which is all 13 year old girls.

People meet me and they are like, I really love your music. It has an impact on my life. But it is not a big deal because they feel like they already know me. There is something about just being yourself and being a regular person that people gravitate towards now.

There is also a danger now because people expect to much. I get emails saying, I really like your music, please send an autographed picture to my address. They write and ask for me to play a show in the park for their girlfriend.

Matt: How important do you think geography is for a new artist?

Kelly: That question depends on so many things.

Brad: I would say it doesn't matter. I grew up in Flower Mound, TX, a suburb of Dallas. I started developing a following online. We came to Nashville because there is no industry in Dallas. Everyone that I talk to is in LA, New York or Nashville. I came here to be closer to business. I didn't come here to break in to the industry.

It is great to be here for networking purposes. Everyone that I met knows someone who knows someone. But how often does that really work? "I met someone who knows someone, and now I am on the cover of Rolling Stone."

Brad: It depends on what you want to pursue. If you are pursuing a record label, you need to be in Nashville because there are record label people. We are pursuing building a fan base. Nashville is not necessarily the place for us.

Matt: Have you pursued a radio campaign?

Brad: We have seen both sides of things because we worked in radio. We used to see people coming to the radio staff and hoping to get their song on the radio.

Kelly: The conference room thing has never worked. I can't think of one time when an artist has gotten a song added from playing to a radio staff.

Brad: You spend $300 on box lunches for everyone. A lot of people just come in the conference room and take the lunch and don't even watch you.

All that it takes to get on the radio is a lot of money. It is still payola. The radio play that we did get, we got a bill for that said "advertising cost." They consider playing your song on the radio as advertising cost.

Kelly: We got added to 18 stations for 3 weeks. In order for your airplay to matter, you have to be on in at least 50 stations for 2 months. People need repetition.

Brad: I was still working at the radio station when MTV happened. I was the #1 artist on MySpace for a year and a half. I told them that they could have the story of breaking a local successful artist. He wanted nothing to do with it. He wants the money.

Kelly: It is ridiculous. I don't know how much they do it now because the labels are running out of money. But, the program directors would get season tickets to the Mavs or the Rangers if they added two new artists this month. Radio stations only have two new artists to be added each week. It is a rotation. Two people get put on, and two get pulled off. Labels buy those spots. They say, when you come here, you get tickets to the Ritz for a week, and the best broadway shows. That is illegal now. So, they just bill you for advertising costs directly.

Matt: What about video?

Kelly: We went to VH1 and played with them. They say that they aren't tied to radio, but I think they are. They say that they add videos before the radio. I haven't really seen that. They were really nice people. They got him on Vh1.com.

Brad: I was on MTV Europe.

Kelly: One of the best things that we have done is a video campaign that was great cheap marketing. $3,000 for a two month campaign. Our video was added to 50 different retail outlets. The campaign was with Hitvideo. That was our number one cheap cost where people came out to shows because they saw a video in some store. That was just something that we did and didn't know how well it was gonna go.

Matt: If you could talk to yourself in 2001 and give yourself advice, what would you say?

Brad: I would probably tell myself not to give up. I have done a lot of cool things. But there are days when you really want to give up. It takes its toll on you driving across the country. Sleeping in vans, eating three-dollar happy meals for breakfast, lunch, and dinner. There is a lot of really cool things that I have done. I'm gonna play in Sun Studio in Memphis this week for the third time. If I had told myself that I was gonna play where Elvis and Johnny Cash got started, I wouldn't have believed it.

Kelly: Especially, if you didn't have a record label. In 2001, that was the main route. People still think it is. They come up to us and say "Hang in there, you will get signed soon."

Brad: The general public thinks that if you are on a record label, then you have a lot of money. They come up to me and say "Those labels are stupid for not signing you man. Keep at it!" It's like, yeah, but I chose that route. It just means that you need to support me and not steal my stuff online.

Griffin House

Matt: When did you start playing guitar?

GH: I bought a guitar from a friend of mine who lived in Springfield, Ohio. I bought it for $100 bucks. I tried to play it a little bit but I got so frustrated that I kicked the strings off of the guitar and never touched again for two years.

I started playing when I was 18 and went away to college. I just wanted to try something new. I guess that's when I started playing guitar. I moved into an artist dorm and a lot of people there knew how to play guitar and piano. I learned a lot from them to get started. I had been writing poetry and stuff before, probably since I had been 14 or 15. So, the words started before the music for sure.

Matt: When was your first public gig?

GH: I joined a band in college called Saint James Gate, which I was sort of coerced into. I didn't even want to do it, but they asked me to be the singer. We played at a place in Oxford called Cachinco. Our first show was totally jam-packed. We had a few rehearsals and a few cover songs worked up that I was really excited about singing. That first gig was so exciting. It was packed and I was addicted from then on. I just wanted to keep going and doing it. So, I did.

Matt: When did you first realize that it was going to be possible to not have to have a day job?

GH: Oh…man. That took awhile. Going back on the timeline with what happened with us in college, I got really serious about music. I really wanted to do it and try as hard as we could. The band was sort of floundering and I said, 'If we don't have a record recorded by the end of the summer, I'm quitting the band. This is ridiculous.'

We were spending, like, two or three days a week driving from Cincinnati up to Oxford to rehearse during the summer. So, we were really dedicated, but just not getting anywhere.

Matt: Did you guys have a manager at that point?

GH: No. It was just really beginning-level stuff. I just decided after awhile when I went away to Europe to study for a semester in Luxembourg . . . we had a branch campus there for the university that I went to and I wrote every night. I recorded stuff walking the streets for the first time around Europe. Just feeling so adventurous and discovering new stuff and dreaming. I wrote a lot of songs over there.

When I came home in the summer I lived in a house with the band in Cincinnati. It was the summer before my senior year of college. I recorded a record of my own songs. I did it on a digital 12 track recorder. One of the guys in the band helped me mix it and put it on to CD form. I took it to school and pressed up a bunch of copies and started selling it to all of my friends, guys I knew in fraternities, people in class (and made teachers mad).

Then, I started playing shows out by myself at Miami. That was my first experience of performing live. I kept doing that and doing that. I kept making recordings and playing as much as I could.

Then, eventually, I moved to Nashville and one thing led to another. One of my demos got in the hands of a record label in New York. All of a sudden I was flying to New York and L.A. and meeting with all of these major labels and talking about deals. It kind of happened pretty quick.

Matt: What was the first major taste of success that you had?

GH: The first really exciting thing that happened for me was, I went to Nashville, I recorded with some friends, some demos. I was working a job for 7 bucks an hour on Broadway in Nashville for several months.

I got a call from a lady at Island/Def Jam records named Diana Fragnito and I flew up to New York and met with her. Then, after everybody else found out that I did that, I got a bunch of calls from a bunch of other labels. So, I flew out to Dreamworks in L.A. and a couple of other labels. That was really exciting to be like 'Oh, man! Finally, there is a possibility to sign a really great deal.' Things just kept snowballing after that.

I think it was just a matter of . . . for me . . . when I look back on it, I just needed to record some songs that got people's attention. Going through the process of recording my own stuff, no matter how good or bad the production was, just getting it down.

Matt: How did the woman at Island/Def Jam find out about your demo?

GH: That's a funny story too. She was meeting with another artist in Nashville, a friend of mine named Dave Barnes. He was up there for a meeting with her because she had just signed (Dave and Griffin's friend) Marc Broussard to Island/Def Jam and so Dave was up there probably meeting to try to get a deal. He gave her my record, like, in the meeting! Just decided, 'Hey, this is a friend that I believe in. You should listen to his music.' So she called me and flew me up there. I kind of owe a lot to that guy because he opened up a bit of a buzz for me at a time when I needed a door to be opened. This was in the Spring of 2003.

Matt: At what point in your career did you first have a manager?

GH: I'm managed by Nettwerk Management. I signed with them in 2004. I flew up to Vancouver and met everybody at the Vancouver office and signed a deal with them. That was kind of a result too of us just doing it on our own.

I had just started a national tour with a band called Over The Rhine that is from Cincinnati. They were huge band for me to open for. I was really excited about it. But two shows into the tour, it got cancelled and I went home with nothing to do, totally discouraged that I was getting ready to finally be on this national tour, that was done now.

But that's when we recorded *Lost and Found*, the first record that I ever put out. That got me my management deal with Nettwerk. They licensed it and put it out. Ever since then, I've just been playing shows and recording music and putting it out. So, it kind of all just happened that way.

Matt: When was the first time you had a music attorney?

GH: The attorney happened a little bit before hand. I remember talking to Lost Highway and I was excited about that label because, before moving to Nashville, I was a huge Ryan Adams fan, and I was talking to Luke Lewis (the guy who runs Lost Highway) on the phone one day. He said, 'We'd really like to do a deal, but we're not going to do anything until you have a lawyer.' So, then I realized that I needed to find a lawyer. So, I talked to tons of lawyers. I met with this guy Jim Zumwalt in Nashville and I just liked him. He was charming and just felt like an old guy that I could trust. He's been a great lawyer for me.

Matt: Do you have a booking agent?

GH: I'm booked by CAA. My agent, Scott Clayton, books John Mayer and My Morning Jacket, and Kings of Leon, and a bunch of other guys.

Matt: What about a publicist?

GH: Right now, I don't have one because we don't have a new record right now. But, I had a publicist called Shore Fire for *Flying Upside Down*.

Matt: So, you only hire a publicist when you have a new record out?

GH: Yeah.

Matt: Did you already register all of your copyrights before you had a lawyer?

GH: He kind of helped me do that. He was really good at that. He helped me get organized and started. To a degree, he was a manager for me before I had a manager.

Matt: You talked about the Over The Rhine tour, was that your first national tour?

GH: That was the first taste that I had of expecting to go out for awhile. But then after that didn't happen, I got my booking deal and my management deal within a matter of months after that. So, the first time that I ever went out on tour I was opening for a CAA band. I was in my car by myself driving myself to all of these shows with my guitar and opening up. Making 13 hour drives a day sometimes just to do it because I wanted it so bad. I would have done anything at that point.

Matt: How do you think you gained your first fans?

GH: I think some of the songs just work for themselves when I'm not working. Once they are out there, the songs are making fans by just being available when you can't do anything about it. I think playing a lot of live shows and having a lot of music out there, slowly but surely, that gets the job done. That's been a slow and steady road.

Matt: You've had success with licensing deals. How did you get your first few licensing deals?

GH: That was something that came along pretty naturally through Nettwerk because they have a really great film and TV department. They've been really good about getting me a ton of TV slots, and a few film slots, and a few commercials. Those have really helped a lot.

Matt: How important do you think Geography is for an artist to make it? Do you need to live in Nashville, New York, or L.A.?

GH: Not anymore. At this point in my career, I don't think it is important where I live. I think it was really important for me to move to Nashville when I first started because I needed to make connections. But, at a certain point, you make connections, and there are really not that many more that you need to make. You just need to start making great records and keep going and keep working hard. I think you can do that from anywhere.

The country is getting smaller and smaller. And the world is getting smaller and smaller too with technology. So, I don't think it is that big of a deal, except for when you are first starting, it is a good idea to be in a good location.

Matt: As a percentage of your income, what is the biggest piece of the pie?

GH: I don't really know to be honest, because up until this point in my life, I have just been scraping by. Finally, this year or last year, I'm like 'Hey! I've got some money in my bank account.' I don't know where it came from. I think part of it is definitely from film and TV, some of it is from touring, selling CDs on the road. I think film and TV has been a big part of it. Obviously, everyone is going to be on that in the future.

Matt: If you were to talk to yourself before you got started, what advice would you give yourself?

GH: Go for it! That's all I would say. Just go for it. Live out of your heart and try not to think to much. Just do it.

Johnny Lee

Matt: How old were you when you started Johnny Lee and the Roadrunners?

JL: I was middle-way through my sophomore year. It was guys in the FFA. They put a band together. There was gonna be a big talent contest between all of the local schools. No one from our school had ever done anything like this. They put a band together and word got out that they were looking for a vocalist.

I used to herd cattle and I knew every word to every song on the radio. I would sing those songs while I was herding cattle. I fell in love with it. I told them I wanted to audition to be the singer and they all thought I was bullshittin' them. Out in the country there wasn't too many singers walking around. I was kind of mischeivious in high school. Either me, or Daryl Phillips or Billy Holder did it, or we knew who did it when it came to trouble.

So, anyway, I went and auditioned at an ol' boy's house named Claud Summerall. They were having band practice and they thought I was bullshittin' them. I showed up and the first song I ever sang was Johnny B. Good, that old Chuck Berry song. I've been singing ever since.

We went on to win the talent contest statewide and everything else too. We started playing for teen hops and different things like that. We would play anywhere to make a few bucks.

Matt: Did you have a strategy for getting your first gigs?

JL: A high school would have a dance or something. There wasn't a lot of bands back then where I lived. We were the only one. Forty or fifty miles away, there was other people that played music. But there wasn't many bands that were worth a shit back then. We were able to be pretty good.

Later on, how we came on to do our first record was a guy by the name of Don Burns, who used to book at the recreation center in Texas City, Texas. He was the one in charge of booking all of the talent. So, my grandfather went with me as my moral support for the first big job that I went to book for the band. As I was sitting in the office, I'll never forget, he said 'We'll what do you guys charge? I've heard of you. So, what do you charge?' It was like five of us. I said, very boldly, 'We won't work for less than five dollars a man.' He said, I'm sorry I can't use you. My heart sank and I said, 'Why?' He said, 'Because we don't pay less than twenty.' I felt like an idiot in front of my grandfather. But that ol' boy ended up being our booking agent and manager so to speak.

Matt: You went in to the Navy after high school, right?

JL: Yeah, after my band broke up and my high school sweetheart's mother made us break up, I had lost my band and I lost my girlfriend, I went to join the Marines. The Marine guy was at lunch, and the Navy guy was across the hall and had all of this shit on his arms and on his chest. I didn't know how long it took to get all that stuff. But, I ended up in his office and he talked me into it.

Matt: Can you tell me about your return to pursuing music after you got out of the Navy? What was the first thing that you did?

JL: I was going to be a highway patrolman. I took my test out in California. But, I changed my mind about that. I didn't want to put on another uniform and have people bark orders at me.

I went and sat in and played drums one night with a group called the Cascades. They had a song called *Listen to the Rhythm of the Falling Rain*. I played drums with them at a club in California. While I was in the military, we had put a little band together too. So, I was playing drums and singing with this little band whenever we had time. Anyway, after that, I was working my ass off building bridges and doing construction. I got tired of that.

So, I put all of my stuff in the back of an old Chevy and drove back to Galveston, Texas non-stop. There, I was working during the day on a dredge boat and doing whatever else I could do. There was another band who had heard that I was back in town. They were looking for a singer. So, I went to sing with them. They had a real lame drummer. So, I tried to sit in on the drums and sing for these guys and show the drummer what to do. They ended up firing the drummer and I bought his drums and was the drummer and the singer for these guys up until the time I met Mickey Gilley.

Matt: So, you weren't signed to any record label with that band, right? You just played around Galveston and Houston?

JL: Yeah. Dickinson, Texas. Our first job was up around there. Houston was big time man! I hadn't made it to Houston yet. But, I made it to Pasadena, Texas, where I met this guy named Mickey Gilley. Hell no, we wasn't signed to a record label! No.

Matt: Can you tell me about how you came in to meeting Mickey Gilley and how all of that got started?

JL: I knew that Mickey Gilley was a big wig up in Pasadena. He was a big star in the Houston area. I went up to see him one night, with hopes of maybe getting to talk to him, and maybe sitting in with his band, hoping that he would like me.

I went up to him and I introduced myself to him and said, I know you don't remember me, but I did a tv show with you in Galveston, Texas a while back. There was a television show called the Larry Cane Show, at the time, it was like Dick Clark's Bandstand. I said 'I was on before you. You came on after me. We didn't have time to stick around. We had a job that night. I heard you was up here and I just wanted to come up and say hi and tell you what a great artist I think you are. I've been listening to your playing and singing.' He said, 'Oh, yeah, yeah.'

So, instead of me asking him if I could sit in and sing, and him having the opportunity to say no, I just acted like I knew him. He ended up asking me if I wanted to sit in with the band. I said, 'sure.' He asked me to sit in with him a few more times. He eventually offered me a job. But, in all reality, I had never seen him before in my life.

Matt: So, he wasn't really on that show with you then?

JL: F*ck no! I didn't even do the show. If I was asking him if I could sit in, then he could always say no. So, I figured that if he thought I was good enough to be on a television show, then maybe he would ask me to play with him. And he did. He was just being courteous. I ended up being the band leader a few months later.

Matt: Did you play an instrument in that band?

JL: I told him that I played horn and guitar and drums. I had a horn player hired for him. He wanted to work with some horns. I hadn't played horn since high school. So, I had to go buy a horn and relearn that shit so that I wouldn't get caught in a lie. I just played whatever needed to be played.

Matt: How did things progress after that with Mickey Gilley? What led to your first record deal?

JL: Well, he was in a partnership with a recording studio in Houston. But, to back up a little bit, I had a record out in high school, so this wasn't my first record.

But, we were drawing crowds and had a kick-ass band. And we were pretty hot shit around the town. So, we would go record records and release them local. We was making a little bit of noise around the Texas and Louisiana area. We kept on recording and recording, trying to find songs. We was gonna make an album so that we could sell it at the shows.

I was just pursuing a recording career man. I didn't know what to record. It was hard to find hit songs because, even today, the songwriters that are writing, they are wanting people to record their songs. So, the better ones are not getting played for everyone and are recorded by the people who are already selling a lot. So, we did a lot of old remakes and got a lot of local airplay.

Later on, we ended up opening up for Gilley's. And we made some noise. I had my first national release called Sometimes on Dot records.

Matt: When did you sign with Dot records?

JL: I never did actually sign with them. That's why I thought my relationship with them wouldn't last very long. I had never even met anybody at Dot. They just took the record and release it and it charted. The first record label I signed to was GRT, even though I had a record out on Dot before that.

I signed with GRT right after Dot, mid Seventies. Right after that song made it in the 20's on the charts. Then, a guy by the name of Nelson Larkin was coming out to Gilley's and had some acts that he had booked at Gilley's. He heard me singing and started talking to the club owner and said they would like to record me. That's how that came about. So, I did an album with GRT called "Here's Johnny."I had three or four mini-hits with them. Never really in the top 10, but the top 20.

I would sing at Gilley's and Gilley's kept growing and growing. Mickey Gilley had a television show that we wrote and produced. That's how the Gilley's club kept getting bigger and bigger. We kept drawing bigger and bigger crowds because we were on tv all the time.

When the guy came along, Andrew Latham, who wrote the article about the legend of the urban cowboy, that is when Paramount Pictures read that and got interested in making a movie. They came out and scouted the place out.

A guy by the name of Irving Azoff, he managed the Eagles, he heard me sing and when it came to do the movie, he asked me if I wanted to do some songs in the movie. I said, 'Hell yeah!'. There was a song that was already recorded called 'Cherokee Fiddle' that caught his attention. Michael Murphy had wrote that song and I redid it. I put my own brand to it.

Cherokee Fiddle came out the first part of 1979 on our own label started by me, Mickey Gilley, and Sherwood Crier. We were big shit in Houston and spent a lot of money with the radio stations and had a television show down there. They were playing our stuff.

When Irving Azoff heard me singing, I said I'd love to do some songs for the movie, but I just needed to get some more songs. So, I redid Cherokee Fiddle, and I found a song called Lookin' For Love and I changed it up a little bit. Up until then, I had been working in the nightclub, every night of my life.

Irving Azoff actually came down to listen to Mickey Gilley. He had never heard of me at the time. But then he found out that I had a lot of local hits and he liked me.

Matt: Do you remember the first time that you had a personal manager?

JL: Yeah, that became a huge lawsuit later on. It was a guy named Sherwood Crier, who actually owned Gilley's. He was my personal manager and Mickey Gilley's personal manager. He had us under a 99 year contract at 50%. That wouldn't have been bad if I had got my 50%, but we ended up getting f*cked out of that.

You've got to remember that all my life I have been working to be able to travel the country to play. And now I have the number one record in the country on the pop charts and I'm traveling all over the country. My dreams were coming true. He said 'I'm gonna make you a millionaire.' I trusted the guy.

It cost me just about all the money that I had in a bank account to pay lawyers, and I got screwed out of all the songs I had written. I never saw any royalty checks from Lookin For Love or anything like that. I got my songs back that I had written, but by that time, all of my money was gone. Since then, I have never had another personal manager, other than Jack MacFadden, who was Buck Owen's manager. Jack owned a booking agency and he was taking 15% from the booking agency and a 10% manager fee. He wasn't doing anything for my career, except having the title of being my manager. So, I leaped over his desk and told him that I was gonna f*ck him up if he didn't tear up the contract. At that point in my life, I had already been screwed over so bad, that I didn't want to get f*cked again. So, right there and then, he dissolved our contract and I have never had another manager since.

Matt: Did you ever have an attorney?

JL: No. I wish I would have. I so recommend it. It is a must. There is so much shit. If I would have known about all that stuff, I might have ended up being an attorney instead of a recording artist. I trusted the people in my stall.

Matt: After all the Urban Cowboy stuff, and after Looking For Love, what has your career path been?

JL: I did quite a few more albums after Lookin For Love and toured. I'm still touring. That is what I do. I go work on the weekends and go out on runs wherever I'm booked. I'm not even signed exclusively with a booking agent because none of them do their jobs like they are supposed to do. They just wait on people to ask for you. But, it has been so long since I have had a hit record that no one asks for me.

I make things happen. I book a lot of the stuff myself because of all of the relationships that I have from before. I go out and hustle jobs where the f*cking booking agents now don't. They don't work the phones like they used to. And if you don't make enough money, they drop your ass. I make all my income now from touring.

Matt: How important is the place you live to making it in music?

JL: I don't think you have to live in Nashville. Although, you are a lot closer to work if you are. I actually think it is important to at least be close. If you go to Nashville, that is where all the songwriters are. You've got to go there and get locked in and make new friends and learn how they do this.

Although, when I lived in Nashville, I got less done than when I didn't because I got taken for granted for living there for awhile. But, for somebody starting out, it is important to be at least close. You need to be where the business is.

Matt: Any tips for radio airplay?

JL: Oh God! Radio stations are run by corporations now. It used to be that you could go to a radio station and become friends with those guys and pick up the phone and call them. They were glad to hear from you. They put you on the air and they played your records.

It's all run by corporations now. Believe it or not, some of them don't have a f*cking clue who I am. The thing that pisses me off the most about radio stations right now is that when you turn it on, it says "The New Country." There are all these people like Merle Haggard and Mickey Gilley, and myself who are still making great music but they won't play us because we are too old.

There are classic stations. But the catch 22 on that is that they play your old stuff only. So, if you give them something new, it isn't classic. So they won't play it. There are some of the smaller stations, where if we release something, they won't play it. But, if I gave a major radio station a record, like Charlie Daniels and I have out right now, they would be taking away air time from some big star right now.

Matt: If you could talk directly to a new artist, what other advice would you give them?

JL: I'd tell them the same thing Loretta Lynn told me the first time that she met me: write. You've gotta write songs. Writing is like working out. The more you do it, the better you get at it. And make sure that your ass is covered. Don't let a record company put you so far into debt that if you don't make them millions of dollars, they will shit can you. That will happen.

Have some representation. Learn something about finances and where to put some money if you are lucky enough to make some so you can take care of yourself later on. Because one day, they will shit can you. It will happen one day.

Look at Alabama. They had a great run. But, it aint happening no more. No matter how good you are. You will get shit canned, so cover your ass. And learn all you can about the music industry.

Erin McCarley

Matt: This book is about going from wanting a career in music to having one. How did you do it?

Erin: I got a guitar and I moved to Nashville right after college. Still, I was just a singer. I just went to a community where there was a network and where people have done it a million times before. There was a formula set up. Obviously, that formula has drastically changed, even from five years ago, just because of the internet.

After singing on country demos, I was trying to find the person who I was supposed to be within that career. I had been mimicking everybody's songs. I didn't really know my own voice yet. So, by trial and error, doing certain demos that weren't really in the genre of my voice, I realized that wasn't me. I got a little frustrated because I wasn't writing full songs yet. I was still relying on singing other people's stuff.

I moved to San Diego to get away and clear my head, figure out who I was and what I wanted to do. Did I really want a career in music? It was kind of a soul-searching year of a lot of time alone. A lot of walks on the beach and a lot of cliché things that actually make you focus in and listen to the voice inside about what you are supposed to do.

I don't know what it was, but literally after a year, inspiration kind of hit. I think I was just listening to some new music. I was going to some live shows that were inspiring. I started writing.

Matt: Tell me about the first trip to Nashville after college and the decision to go to Nashville.

Erin: Initially, I wanted to quit college two years in and go to Nashville. I knew one person in the industry [in Nashville] through church or something. I don't even remember what it was. But, that's why it was Nashville and not L.A. or New York.

I didn't grow up in country music. When I got to Nashville that is all that I found myself in. It didn't resonate with me. I liked the music, but it wasn't me. So, I got a little frustrated. Now, I am part of a music community in Nashville that is way far away from country music and is its own indie rock movement. [At the time that I first went to Nashville], I think that was there, but it was just starting. I didn't find it when I was there.

Matt: What were your first steps to get involved in the music industry once you were in Nashville?

Erin: My part-time job helped me to meet people. Right when you are starting, it is good to put yourself in a position of service, whether it is retail or restaurant. It is so cliché, but it is true. I worked at Starbucks. I worked at this furniture store where a lot of designers came for interior design. All of these wives of music execs in the town were coming through. I met this one wife, who happened to be the wife of a publisher in town, Jodi Williams.

Jodi is now my greatest mentor. I've known him for six or seven years. Meeting him and having people like that speak truth into your life and telling you things that you don't want to hear. That was huge. I had two people like that in my life: Jodi and this woman from L.A. that was also on the publishing side, which is the songwriting side.

My angle at beginning a career was focused on the songwriting. I had the initial reaction that a lot of people had when they start doing music of wanting to play shows and get on the road because it seems so exciting. But that is not always the best-case scenario. I think it works for some people. Some people automatically hit the road and it becomes this grass-roots thing where it evolves all at once. For me, I needed more of an isolated songwriting safe-haven.

Matt: When you were singing on demos in Nashville, were they demos to promote you as a solo artist or were they for other people?

Erin: It first started to make money. I quickly made some friends in the industry who were songwriters and needed their songs demoed. So, I did demos for the writer to pitch to an artist. Once I met Jodi, he said "We've got to get you some songs if you're not gonna write them." So, I would go with him to a publisher and look through their catalog and listen to them and think 'Can I sing this? Does it make sense for me?'

I met with Tony Brown one time, who runs Universal South. I went to his office, played him the stuff and thought 'Is this gonna be my moment to get a record deal?' He looked and me and was like 'I love your voice. It is not country at all. Why are you doing this?' He looked at me with this wisdom of 'Keep going. But why are you doing *this*?' This isn't the right path.

Matt: Were those your own songs or another person's songs that you played him?

Erin: This was with country-pop songs. I don't think I've ever told that whole story in an interview before. That was a really bum moment because you work yourself up to thinking that that could be what you are supposed to be doing. I just hadn't found myself yet.

Matt: How did you get the Tony Brown meeting set up? Was this an opportunity that came from you meeting this guy's wife in . . .

Erin: . . . In a furniture store. And her saying, 'You've gotta meet my husband. He would love you.' She hadn't heard me sing. But she just liked our communication together. I was like 'What is publishing? I don't even know what you are talking about.' She was like 'It has to do with the songwriting.' I was like 'Okay?' Of course, I would take any opportunity.

Matt: Before you met Jodi Williams through his wife, were you doing anything else in Nashville music-wise?

Erin: I wasn't trying to play out because I had nothing to play, especially in Nashville. Nashville is a songwriter place. If you are going to play at the bluebird you can't go up there and play a cover song.

Matt: What happened when you left Nashville for San Diego?

Erin: When I moved to San Diego I didn't know if I wanted to do music at all. Jodi was like, 'You've got to do this, but I just don't know what to do with you. You've got to find yourself. I can only do so much.' So, when I went to San Diego I decided not to think about music. If it surfaces, great. But, my plan was to clear my head. I followed a boy there.

I worked at this little boutique on the beach. Women would come in and we would get to talking and they would ask 'What do you do other than this?' I would say music. But, I wasn't going home at night doing anything that had to do with music. But, I would wake up at 4 A.M. thinking why am I not doing music. What is it gonna take?

Matt: So, you really got serious about writing when you went to San Diego.

Erin: Once I left Nashville and was in San Diego and I started writing, I met this other mentor in L.A., Kathleen Carey, through a mutual friend. She was the V.P. of Sony Music. I was intimidated as hell. These were the first songs that I had ever written and I was going to play them for her and see what she thinks. A mutual friend set us up and said "Hey, I think you really need to meet her. She will really like you and she'll tell you straight-on what you need to do." So, I went up there one time, played my songs. She smiled. We spent seven hours together and went to dinner. She was son encouraging. But at the end of the night I'm thinking in my head, 'So, are you gonna give me a publishing deal?' She said "You have so much potential. Go home and keep writing." It was naïve, but necessary.

So,I just stayed home and wrote. While I was doing that I did have a part-time job, but on the in-betweens, that is all that I did. I really isolated and stayed disciplined. On days when I didn't work, I didn't get out of my pajamas. I would just stay at home and write from eight to eight. Sometimes by the end of the night I would have nothing. Sometimes I would have one verse. It was usually a lot of nothing, but it all evolved in to something.

I kept in touch with Jodi Williams (in Nashville) through that whole thing and would send him songs when I thought I had progressed a little bit. So, that's how that went.

Matt: And how did you meet Kathleen again?

Erin: Through a mutual friend in Nashville the first time that I moved to Nashville.

Matt: So that was just another random person that you met who told you about a friend they had in L.A. who was a big wig at Sony?

Erin: It was a songwriter friend of mine in Nashville, she and her twin sister. We became great friends. Kathleen acted as their mentor. They heard a couple of songs that I was doing.

Matt: How did you make that first group of friends when you moved to Nashville?

Erin: When I moved to Nashville, I didn't have a place to live. So for the first week, I lived in a hotel. I didn't know anyone except for this man who was married and had a family, so it wasn't like I could move in with him. So, my boyfriend at the time's college friend's brother lived in Nashville. He called him and asked if he knew anyone who needs a roommate. The guy in Nashville's roommate was leaving and there was an extra room in the house.

So there were two guys with an extra room, and I moved in. They were part of a group of friends that had a lot of songwriters in the group. And some creative people. One of the guys was a painter. In moving in with them, and in hanging with their circle of friends, I met people. And Nashville is small, especially when you start talking music. It all collides. Even with the geography, everybody is within twenty minutes of each other. So, it is really easy to meet people.

Whereas, with San Diego, I think it was good for me because I could isolate and not be distracted because everyone is spread out. I lived in the suburbs, which was not creative at all, but very real estate focused and glossy. So, I think that helped me retract and look inward and figure it out. Whereas, in Nashville I was being more social and fluttering around.

So, that's how I met those people.

Matt: How did you meet up with Jamie?

Erin: Same group of friends, the two sisters who introduced me to Kathleen. They were singer/songwriters as well. They had done a project ten years back where Jamie did some programming for it. They were like 'Hey, we have this guy who is really wanting to get involved with developing an artist from square one. We think you should meet up with him.'

When I was in town settling up some stuff with the first producer, Jamie and I talked around the subject and got to know each other a little bit. I definitely wasn't ready to jump into something because I was kind of burnt from the first thing and didn't want to commit. It sounds like I'm talking about a boyfriend, doesn't it? That's how it is though. It's such a personal business.

But, we went to dinner and had a great vibe. I went back home to San Diego. He had put together a band for a label and was coming up to L.A. to watch their first show together. So, he invited me to come up to L.A. and hang out with him and bring my guitar and play any songs that I wanted to play for him, just so that he knew where I was coming from.

We were at Venice Beach. We went out to the beach with the sun setting, and sat on a bench. I played the beginnings of some of the songs that are on the record. He asked what I saw the songs doing and music that I was listening to and what I grew up on. Then he told me what he saw and I was like, 'Wow, you just said it so much bigger, but exactly like what I was thinking in my head.'

He said 'Come to Nashville and spend a week. I'm not gonna charge you anything. Just get there. We'll work out the details later." So, he gathered up musicians that he thought would work for my album. He didn't get the typical studio musicians. He got some young guys that were eager and willing to do it for cheap and that were on the cutting edge of rock music in Nashville.

We went, and the first song that we did was Pony.

Matt: The same recording of Pony that ended up on the record?

Erin: Yeah. Then, the second one was sleepwalking. We did two songs in that week. It was the perfect match. I had no money. He had no money really. He was gonna give his time, but I had to figure out how in the world we were gonna keep recording. So, I raised money.

I went back to people in my life, who over the years, like the night of graduation of college where the parents are like 'if you need anything and are ever stranded on the side of the road, call me' – type thing. I remembered a couple of families distinctly who said they were there for me and called them. Within two days I had twenty grand. They said, 'We don't need it back.'

So, I had the twenty grand after footing a little bit of the bill myself for the first two songs. Then, we were able to do ten songs, with no label, no manager, no publicist, no nothing. Me and Jamie worked for two years. Pony and everything happened in November 2006.

I went back and forth from San Diego to Nashville for the next six months and did five songs. They had to be so sparse because it was on Jamie's time. He was doing it for free and it was when I could get out there. We gathered the same musicians that we had from day one. Then, I moved to Nashville in July 2007 to finish the record and do the last five songs. There was one song that we did after I signed.

Matt: You were signed after appearing in a showcase at South By Southwest. What did you do to create buzz to get A&R people to come to your showcase? How did you even draw people to your MySpace page to have them come across it?

Erin: I don't know. I put Pony and I put Pitter-Pat, and Love, Save The Empty up on MySpace.

It was just word of mouth because I had lived in San Diego and started doing shows towards the end in L.A. at Hotel Café. Once I posted it on MySpace, talk started happening in those circles, and with the people that I had met in Nashville. The tentacles ventured out and my friends who knew A&R guys were telling them to go to my MySpace page.

All of a sudden, I started getting a call here or a call there from different label A&R guys, from different publishers, a radio guy from KCRW in L.A., who wanted to play Pitter-Pat. So, I compiled this list of all of the people that contacted me.

At this point, Jodie Williams was a V.P. at BMI, who has a showcase at SXSW. So, I called Jodie and asked 'Why am I on BMI?' The best opportunity available for ASCAP or BMI is to help you get on festivals because they have these showcases at Sundance, SXSW, whatever. So, I told Jodie, 'You have to get me on a showcase at SXSW. Help me.' He pushed and pushed and pushed, and a million people are trying to get these showcases, he somehow got me on one.

So, part of that twenty grand that I raised, I took a few grand and put together a band, rented a van and a trailer, and we went down to SXSW. I shot an email to all of those people who were on the contact list and said, 'Hey, I'm playing. Come if you want. This would be a good time to see me. I know you are gonna have people down there.' So, I got there and played. I didn't know if people were gonna show up, but they all did. They all saw each other there. And, it made it seem like 'Who is this girl if he's there?' It created a competition, buzz. No one knew why they were there. They had just heard three songs on MySpace. No one knew if it was gonna suck, or what it was gonna be like. It was a really fun show. Everyone was in good spirits.

The day before I left for SXSW, Kathleen Carey said 'You need a lawyer. If something happens down there, people are gonna start calling you. Start out there." So, she got her friend, Ried Hunter. They came down to SXSW. That next day, I sat in this hotel lobby for seven hours and had meeting after meeting from that.

Matt: With record labels?

Erin: With record labels. It really was like the dream of SXSW. I met my manager there, which I didn't know that he was gonna be my manager. After that night, Michael called and said let's meet. We met at 1:30 in the morning at the Driscoll Hotel. Everyone was partying and he was stone cold sober. I was like 'What am I doing? This is crazy. I don't understand what is going on.' He was like, 'Hey, come to New York.' Then, Universal Republic was like, 'Hey, come to New York.' Then, Columbia was like 'Hey, come to New York.'

About a month and a half of New York, L.A., Chicago, I flew back and forth and met Rick Rubin in Malibu at his house. His dog humped Jamie's leg the entire time. It was just this crazy soirée and swirl. I just wrote some songs that I am proud of, and me and Jamie were sitting in the studio hunched over a piano trying to make it sound the best we could, then that happened.

Matt: If you could speak directly to yourself when you had to do it all over again and were starting today, what would you say?

Erin: I don't want to lead anyone astray. If I could do it over again. . . It is really hard to say. Part of me wants to say forget college and dive into the creative thing. Get a part time job in a city where there is a really tight community of musicians, where it is supportive and positive. Part of me says do that.

But, as a senior in college, I was not ready emotionally to deal with the songs that needed to be written, or just the business in general. So, each step is important. You have to have patience, or else you are going to burn out really fast. I think I am an encouragement to people because I am thirty years old and I just started writing songs five years ago.

Some of the best advice I got was from Jodie and Kathleen saying don't be in a hurry to get out on the road and haphazardly go for it. Sit down. Make a plan. Write some songs that, when you go out on stage, you feel 100% perfect with playing everynight, because you are going to if that is what is going to happen. It is a little more grueling doing that process, but I wouldn't take back the time that was allotted for that. And, just the process of being able to figure out who I was.

Jerry DePizzo (O.A.R.)

Matt: When did you start playing sax?

Jerry: In 5th grade. I was 10 years old. I originally wanted to play the drums, but we had way too many drummers in the school band. The director of the band told me I should play the trumpet, so I went home and told my mom I was going to play trumpet. She told me that one of my uncle's had an extra saxophone. So, I was going to play saxophone. That was it. That's why I played sax. I came up through the public school system learning how to play.

I met the guys in 97 and they already had all the other instruments. I kind of knew how to play. It just went from there.

Matt: What year were you in college when you started playing with Ordinary Peoples and O.A.R.?

Jerry: I played with O.A.R. first. I started sitting in with O.A.R. end of fall quarter freshman year. Then, I slept on Marc's couch for a chunk of that summer after freshman year in Maryland. And then, that Fall of 1998 was when Ordinary Peoples started.

Matt: How did you meet the guys in O.A.R.?

Jerry: Chris and Marc lived in Morell tower together. Marc was actually one of the first guys I met in college. We were all involved in the SAM house on campus in one way, shape or form, during freshman year of 97-98. We were friends. It was mostly just hanging out in the dorms and being buddies. Trying to win girls over with acoustic guitars.

Matt: So, Marc and all of the guys from Maryland started the band in high school, right?

Jerry: There was various incarnations of O.A.R. But those 4 guys started in 96. They recorded the first record in the Spring of 96. That is when they started doing The Wanderer.

Matt: How big was O.A.R. in terms of CD sales and touring when they came to OSU?

Jerry: In 1997, they were like the high school band that your friends had. There wasn't a regional or national O.A.R. It was 4 guys that played their local coffee shop and then went to college.

It started at OSU, just playing anything and everything. House parties, throwing house parties. Mecca, which isn't around anymore. Eventually, the Newport became the hub. It was mainly that we would throw parties in town.

The band was fortunate in that they came from an area in Maryland where everyone dispersed to go to college. So, a lot of their closest friends took a box of CDs with them. They went to Arizona, or the university of Maryland, or Wisconsin. All these different schools. And took the cds with them and sold them out of their dorm rooms. Clemson was another place.

Fall quarter, people were calling them asking for more cds because they had sold out. It really spread that way, through word of mouth.

Matt: There are a lot of good band out there that will have fans show up to shows, who are usually their friends, and then maybe eventually their friends' friends. A lot of times, those kind of bands reach a wall where they can't get more than 30-40 fans at a show. What did O.A.R. do to promote its music initially and connect with fans? What separated O.A.R. from other bands?

Jerry: I think what really separates O.A.R. is the songs and the songwriting, the lyrical content. O.A.R. sounds a little different than everyone else. It may sound a little like this band and a little like that band, but it is recognizable as O.A.R. The songwriting is good. People really connect with the tunes that we write and what Marc has to say. People enjoy our music and it makes them feel good. I don't think there is any crazy formula to it. It is not rocket science. But we make people feel good when we play music.

Matt: So you guys didn't have any master plan for fan growth?

Jerry: We were smart about it. We were fortunate because we had Marc's brother, Dave Roberge, at the helm steering the business side of the ship. He was a sharp guy and he learned as trial by fire. He went to Florida. Graduated from Florida in 98. He was working at a job in Vegas. The guys called him at first and asked to help book some shows and look over proposals. Dave left his job and moved back to Florida with his fiancé and future wife and ran O.A.R. out of an apartment in Florida before he got married and moved back to Maryland and eventually to New York.

We were smart about our opportunities. O.A.R. never played a show for 5 people. It was always packed houses. The live thing is really what it centered around. People always gravitated towards the live shows and had a great time at the shows.

We didn't go and play Columbus one weekend, New York the next, West Virginia the next, and then, Florida. We had a concentrated effort. It was Columbus. Then, Columbus and Athens. Then, Columbus, Athens, Cleveland. Then, Columbus, Athens, Cleveland, Toledo. Then Columbus, Athens, Cleveland, Toledo, Miami (OH). It was an hour radius, then two hours, four hours, and six hours.

Matt: When you first started playing with the band, had they already started to tour outside of Columbus?

Jerry: They had played a couple shows at The Grand Marquis in Maryland, which is like a coffee shop that you and your high school buddies would go to and just hang out and be stupid. They and their friends would go there and play shows. They opened up for Mark's brother's band, Foxtrot Zulu, and Maryland once. But, there was no O.A.R. as you know it today. It was just a bunch of buddies with a cd that they duplicated at discmakers.

Matt: But, that first CD had Crazy Game of Poker.

Jerry: It had Crazy Game of Poker.

Matt: What do you think it is about that song that made it so massive?

Jerry: People sing the hell out of that song. They had the country part mapped out at the beginning, and they knew that they wanted to make the reggae part at the end. What

Marc came up with off the top of his head in the studio when they hit record the one time they recorded it was where the lyrics and everything just stuck. That was it. Maybe that spontaneity or that innocence connected with people.

It goes back to "it makes people feel good." If you are asking what seperates us from other bands. That is a part of it too. Every band has that one tune they are known for. Ours is that song. I imagine that at two o'clock in the morning at bars across the country, that song is being played in a couple of places.

Matt: When you are going through a new town, how did you decide what venues to play and what towns to play?

Jerry: Pretty early on, we had a street team presence. We had volunteer kids who were just fans. We utilized independent record stores a lot. Johnny Go's house of music is a place here in Columbus that was a big one. It was the first place the band went to sell their CDs on consignment.

I think Dave bought a book with a list of all the clubs and venues. He would look through and see that First Run in Miami (OH) has a capacity of 700 people. He would just call and say, "Hi, we are O.A.R. We would like to play." Maybe we would have to go open up for a band the first time.

The place would be jam packed when we played and then the headliner would go on.

Matt: A lot of the other artists that have been interviewed for this book have had a "lightning strikes moment." It doesn't seem like O.A.R. had a lightning strikes moment. Did they?

Jerry: If you ask me, that never existed. There was never a point when one day we were X and the next day we were 10X. It was really a steady gradual build for years and years and years. There are certain things that have helped. If there was one, it was that when the band recorded the first record, they recorded Poker. That was the song that caught people's ear and got them in to the music. Having Dave involved was a big part of it. Dave at some point 98-99 went in to Warner Brothers and sat down with some of the suits. He said "Here is the business model. Here is the band. Here is what we are doing on our own." He was able to get a P&D deal with them to start a record label. Everfine. Before we even got a record deal we sold 100,000 records.

We had a booking agent, Brian Manning, was a guy at CAA that saw us and signed us at Clutch Cargo in Grand Rapids, MI. He wasn't even an agent at that point. He was just an assistant. Later on, we went with Chip Hooper at Monterey, which is now Paradigm.

Matt: When did you realize that you would be able to be a full time musician and not have to get another job?

Jerry: For me, it was in 2000. August/September of 2000. We played the House of Blues in Chicago and sold it out three nights in a row. For a kid from Youngstown, Chicago might as well be New York and Hong Kong wrapped in to one. I was like “Holy shit! I’m going to be able to quit my job.”

Actually, I quit my job in July 2000. The band left college in 2001. Marc and Chris graduated in 2001. Rich and Benj and I still had a year left and we still have a year left.

I had a job for a little while. Fall quarter, I got a job at a BP, the one on Lane Avenue. I had that job til I went to a party and some chick was like, “Hey! You’re the BP guy!” So, I quit my job the next day because I didn’t want to be the BP guy.

I sold aluminum siding door to door in the ghettos of Columbus, which was a horrible idea. So, I had this shitty job and was playing sold out shows. But, I wasn’t a member of the band then. So, I would do a month of shows and get like, $150. I wasn’t getting paid well by any means. They didn’t have to pay me. I was just psyched to be up there playing music.

I also waited tables for a couple of years. I worked at Brio. I quit that in July 2000. It’s not like I was raking in dough. But, if I buy groceries instead of going out to eat, and I steal beer instead of buying it, then I will be able to make my car payment and rent. That's basically what I did.

Matt: You joined the band in 2000 at Ohio U, right?

Jerry: Right. They introduced me and the next song we played was Hey Girl.

Matt: Did anyone else approach you for a record deal before you signed with Atlantic?

Jerry: We had interest and we were courted for years really. We spent at least 18 months getting wined and dined by record companies before we signed with, what at that time was Lava. Out of all the labels that courted us, MCA, Capitol, Universal, Lava, others, we had a meeting with all of them. They all wanted to sign us for various reasons. We went with Lava. Jason Flom ran Lava at that time. He was like "Look, I don't want to screw with the music. I just want to sell your records." We liked that.

Matt: What is the most unexpected thing about success as an artist?

Jerry: For me, being young and naïve, I thought, you get in a band. You make a record. Then, you are rich and famous. And that it happened in that order and it took about that long. Obviously, that is not the case. In our case, the amount of legwork that it took and takes, and the fact that your best isn't necessarily what is needed. You need to go above and beyond.

It is surprising to me how much we are still working today. We are always trying to improve and get better and develop. The amount of time that it took to realize and continue that is what shocked me the most.

Anyone that has a record deal can tell you that getting a record deal is square one. It is not the brass ring that you would think it would be when you don't have one.

Matt: When you are playing for a packed arena and packed amphitheater, what is going through your head? Do you ever look out at the crowd and think "This is wild?"

Jerry: Really seldom. In the early days, yes. I was wide-eyed and really impressed by it all. Now, its more, "How do I win them over?" How do I control the situation? How do I make them have a great time and want to come back again? While thinking about what I am supposed to be doing, which is playing music.

Matt: Today, there are all kinds of avenues to reach fans and much of that is through social networking and social media. What are your thoughts on Napster for the band in the early days and social media now as it pertains to connecting with fans?

Jerry: We are in a really exciting time. When it comes to social networking, digital media, whatever you want to call it, it is the Wild West. Napster, for us was a great resource in the beginning. It is kind of a double-edged sword now. We are one of those bands that people gravitated towards and really sparked an interest. Through no doing of our own, people traded and downloaded OAR's music off of Napster. But, that may have trained them to not buy our music when it was readily available in stores and when they heard it on the radio and there became avenues online to fill that instant gratification of buying it when you hear it. But, it certainly got our music out to places where we were not able to get it through traditional means of record stores, TV, and all those kinds of things that we have now, 13 years later. So, in the beginning, valuable resource. Right now, double-edged sword.

But, at that point, 12 years ago, Itunes, Rhapsody, Facebook, and Myspace didn't exist. It was just Napster.

I think Twitter is really cool. I find it very therapeutic to be honest with you. To send out what you are thinking at that very second to whoever wants to listen. I think it is kind of cool. I don't receive anyone else's twitter. I just throw mine out and see what sticks. There are some people who are great at that stuff and some who aren't. John Mayer is great at that. He is a witty, funny, dude. His tweets are funny. It's good stuff. Me, I'm "sitting on the couch, wondering what to tweet." It is a great way to reach people, and is a really cool idea to follow whoever the biggest star in the world is and see what they are thinking. Pretty sharp.

Matt: In the past, people would bring posters to shows to be able to communicate with the artist by having them see the sign in the crowd. Now, assuming the artist checks their own account, you can communicate directly with the artist by referencing their name.

Jerry: I think it is super cool. I didn't know that until 6 months after I started tweeting. Then, Benj taught me about it. Mark was really sharp about it. We had this twitter co-writing contest. We picked a verse, chorus, and bridge to write this tune that we are going to give out to charity or use for something. It is called Lightswitch Sky.

Matt: If you were starting from square one today, what advice would you give to yourself, assuming that they have the skills and the songs, and are above the talent threshold (capable of taking it to the next level)?

Jerry: It depends on the situation that you are in. If you are in a band like O.A.R. and people are coming to the shows, keep doing it on your own for as long as you can, until a great or lucrative opportunity comes your way. What helped O.A.R. the most is that we were able to do so much legwork on our own that the labels could come in and take us to the next level. Do as much as you can on your own. Educate yourself. When you are going to sign and bring other people in, make sure that there are like-minded individuals who share the same goals values as you do and you feel comfortable with them. Our A&R guy is someone who I could take my family over to their house and hang out, same with business manager and booking agent. This has helped me and the guys convey what we would like to see.

Chris Trapper

Matt: When did you first know that you wanted a career in music?

Chris: There were two stages. First, the fantasy stage of sneaking into an empty auditorium and singing and imagining that the seats were full and they were clapping for me. Then, later on, actually realizing that I could do it for a living.

Matt: When did you begin playing?

Chris: I started playing open mics at a coffee house in Boston that was really a poetry slam place. Then, I got hooked up with a well-known singer/songwriter in Boston who helped me get gigs.

I also played in a few bands, but it wasn't professional. Would have one gig every six months, but they thought we were going to be the next U2.

Matt: How did The Push Stars form?

Chris: I was at a show at The Middle East in Boston and saw Ryan MacMillan playing with someone else. I talked to him after the show about playing together some time and it went from there. Our bass player started out as a session player when Ryan and I were doing a demo. He sounded good and we thought it made sense to make him a full time member of the band,

Eventually, we recorded a demo and played gigs in Boston. After awhile, people started coming to our shows and we got a manager. That manager had a relationship with IMAGO records. So we were able to sign a deal to IMAGO for a one record. That manager also knew Rosemary Carroll, a big time entertainment lawyer who agreed to shop our demo to major labels.

We ended up going with another manager though. At the time the demo was being shopped by Rosemary Carroll, our second manager knew The Farrely Brothers and got a placement in the movie *There's Something About Mary*. So, it made the labels more interested in us because we already had a placement in a major film that was coming out. That helped a lot.

Later, we played a showcase in New York where 16 labels showed up. It was pretty crazy. We were offered deals by Columbia Aware, Arista, and Capitol. We took the deal with Capitol because their president, Gary Gersh, met with us and took interest. We liked him.

Matt: At the beginning of The Push Stars, before you were signed to a major label, how did you approach touring? Was it just regional around Boston?

Chris: At first, we had a local guy in Boston help us out with booking. But, we didn't really have a concrete strategy for booking our shows. What we did is probably an example of what not to do.

We would play a show in Pittsburgh one night and drive back for an AIDS walk in Boston the next day, literally risking our lives to be there on time. It doesn't make sense to play gigs in places where you have not been asked to play. Make sure people are going to show up and want to see you play in cities where you book gigs.

Matt: Why did The Push Stars end their relationship with Capitol Records?

Chris: There were changes at the record label with the management and A&R. Gary Gersh, who signed us and was a big part of why we signed with Capitol, left and the new team came in. The Push Stars survived the new group of management, but eventually we were dropped from Capitol due to creative differences.

We wrote fifty songs and recorded the demos and the label asked another writer to come in and do some co-writing with me. I didn't really connect creatively with that co-writer and I thought that the fifty songs that we worked on had plenty of material that the label could have released.

We weren't making enough money on Capitol to justify us having a legacy as sell-outs and for us to not make the kind of music that we wanted to make. It wasn't the easiest thing to do, but after awhile we knew that we were not on the same page as the label and when we told the label that, they dropped us.

Matt: Did you ever have a "lightning strikes moment" with The Push Stars or in your solo career, or has everything just been a slow and steady build?

Chris: There have been lots of little lightning strikes. It all started out with me quitting my job. None of this would have happened if I didn't get serious about going after music. I had some encouragement from people around me and I listened to them.

Then, early on with The Push Stars, we had a couple of managers with some important industry connections. Rosemary Carroll got labels to pay attention to us and then the placement in *There's Something About Mary* helped us to solidify that interest.

And being signed to a major label in and of itself was a lightning strike for our indie career. We got a lot of exposure from being on Capitol. A lot of my fans today are fans because they heard of The Push Stars from us being on Capitol.

We had another big break with the Matchbox Twenty tour. Greg Collins, the guy who engineered our record, Paint The Town, also did some studio work with Matchbox Twenty. Greg gave Rob Thomas a raw mix of the tracks from Paint The Town and Rob liked the record a lot. He asked us to come out on tour and open up for Matchbox Twenty on an arena tour. He was so supportive and watched all of our sets from the side of the stage.

Rob and the guys in Matchbox really took a chance on us because it didn't meet any of the rules for an opening band for an arena tour. We weren't on a major label. We didn't have a video on VH1 or a radio single. Somehow, we were still able to do it and it was a great experience.

I've also had a lot of movie and tv placements that ended up helping out and reaching new fans.

So, there wasn't one key event. There were a lot of sustained little ones.

Matt: What is the most unexpected thing about success as an artist that you have experienced so far?

Chris: That people want to meet me. That people come up to me after the shows with trembling hands sometimes because my music has affected them. It's not from an ego level, but just from a standpoint of knowing that your music has an effect on someone's life. I didn't expect that and it always makes me feel great and thankful.

Matt: You have transitioned from dealing with labels to having complete control of your career. How was that transition?

Chris: It has been amazing. Of course, there are ups and downs. Having an independent music career is just like owning a pizza shop. You don't know where your next customers are going to come from. Sometimes I don't know where the money is going to come from.

The Push Stars had a serious dry spell before the Matchbox Twenty tour. We didn't have any film or TV placements and weren't making a lot of money. And then we got a major boost. In my solo career, I've had dry spells and then I get big boosts from things like placements in *Devil Wears Prada* and

August Rush. It is always up and down, but I love playing the solo acoustic shows.

Also, the thing about touring as a solo act is that I can tour in some places where I have never played before, but if you have enough really enthusiastic fans, those fans will bring people. I just had a great show in Hickory, North Carolina because there were three or four really big fans who all brought a bunch of people and the place was packed.

In San Diego, I played a bummer show for about fifteen people once, which I thought was a failure. But after that show, I met a lady there who booked me for a house concert the next time I was in town. That house concert turned into another even bigger house concert the next time in San Diego. Now, when I play clubs in San Diego, I have a great turn out, based mostly from the House concert buzz.

My crowds vary in every city. A lot of people are fans from the Push Stars, but there are also a lot of people who are new fans and heard me in movies and tv. It's been a great career and I love doing it for a living.

Matt: What social networking site do you use and what are your thoughts on fan interaction and developing a fan base?

Chris: The individual social media site will keep changing, but all that matters is getting fans. When people ask me what is the first thing you should do as a musician, after writing great songs and being a great performer to have a career. The answer is easy. Get fans.

Myspace has kind of fizzled out and now Facebook is the thing. But real fans will follow you wherever you go. Build fans. Have real interactions with them. That's the difference between me and a big star like John Mayer. I am a person who meets with the fans and talks to them after the show. And, hopefully, they can walk away saying "this guy is not a dick."

Matt: What advice would you give to a new artist who does not have any contacts in music to begin networking? How do you "network" without looking like a jerk?

Chris: Take that word "networking" and never use it again. Just be real and talk to people and be cool. I can tell when people are being genuine and when they are being an opportunist. Someone like Rob Thomas, who deals with a thousand people a day, has an unbelievable bullshit detector. He can tell right away whether someone is genuine. Just be a real person.

Saving Jane/Marti Dodson

Matt: When did you first know that you wanted a career in music?

Marti: I think it was something that was always on the backburner for me. I had been singing and I started writing songs pretty early, but my parents insisted that I go to school and get a degree. So, I did both at the same time and really got serious about it when I was 18 or 19 and in college.

Matt: What did you do to get serious about it?

Marti: I had been in a couple bands as a background singer. Then, I met up with a guy that I am still in a band with today at a campfire party. We decided to form a band and started recording. So that was one of the first things, just putting some of the ideas that I had down in the studio and just getting up there and playing.

Matt: Were you a singer and guitar player, or just a singer at that time?

Marti: I've never been a guitar player. I can play chords well enough to write songs. And that is what I did.

Matt: Did you guys record first or start playing live first?

Marti: We did record first. We actually had gigs booked before we had a name. We recorded mostly just acoustic demos, like guitar and vocal. Then, we were like, this is kind of fun. We should have a band. And we started from there.

Matt: When you first started playing out live were you playing covers?

Marti: We were pretty much a cover band at first. Our goal was to play covers to make money to fund the recording of originals. We were 75/25 covers to originals at first.

Matt: Around what year was the first time you recorded as Saving Jane?

Marti: 2002.

Matt: Home studio or professional studio?

Marti Workbook studios in Columbus.

Matt: When did you start playing gigs outside of Columbus?

Marti: Not until we had a song on the radio. We didn't hit the road until Girl Next Door came out.

Matt: What was your first interaction with Toucan Cove? When did it go from being a local thing to a national thing?

Marti: We had a relationship with WNCI, the top 40 station in Columbus. We used to always do their Buckeye Bashes across the street. We recorded our first local independent release. I gave it to the program director there. He liked it. He hooked me up with Mark Liggett, who became our manager. That was in 2004. We started recording with Mark and did a couple of small EPs with him. He had a relationship with Toucan Cove, which is an indie label that we are still signed to. He set that up with them and we got the deal with Toucan Cove.

Put out Girl Next Door in 2005. It seems like so long ago, but it really wasn't. Girl Next Door was on the radio in early 2006. At that time, we got picked up by Universal Republic and did an album with them.

Matt: What was your connection with WNCI?

Marti: The drummer was good friends with the station, so we got the gig as the house band, which was a cover show before games. Everyone was drinking and partying, and we were playing *Hang On Sloopy*.

Matt: So, it was a person in your band, who had a connection to WNCI, who had a connection to Mark Liggett, who had a connection to Toucan Cove?

Marti: Right. And Mark managed Blessid Union of Souls back in the Nineties. He had that history and was a big dance record producer in the early Nineties. He is also from Ohio and lives in Cincinnati, which was a nice fit for us.

Matt: Did Mark have a specific reason for choosing Saving Jane?

Marti: The songwriting and the marketability of a female fronting band. Mark is very much image conscious more than other managers.

Matt: How did radio play start with Girl Next Door?

Marti: We actually put that song out five times. It wasn't overnight or anything like that. The first station that played us was in South Bend Indiana. I remember going up there to do a show and nobody knows who we are anywhere else in the country. But we get there to this little town and people are lined up to see us. They were like "Oh my God! You are Saving Jane!" and I was like "What?!"

That was a really cool thing, but it was so isolated to that area. Radio is weird like that. There are some places in the country where everyone knows who we are. There are other places where people are like "Who?"

It started with the Midwest, from the ground up. Then, it really built up in the Midwest. Radio is difficult to explain quickly. But the way that it works is they do all kinds of research on the songs that they play, and there are different ways to determine if they are going to continue to play something, aside from the relationships that they have with the record labels.

But that song just wouldn't go away. It just kept researching well and kept getting call ins. And when you can prove that to other stations, they will start to add it. So, then we had a few more stations add it. The biggest thing that made it tip over the edge was Z100 picked it up in New York. Then all of the other stations picked it up.

Matt: Did you notice a bump after Toucan Cove was bought by Universal?

Marti: Actually, that is when it started to decline. The song had been out for 6-7 months at that point. Universal was in the process of splitting into Universal MoTown and Universal Republic. No one was working the record and it kind of fizzled out after that.

Matt: What is the most unexpected thing that happened to you about having a song on commercial pop radio?

Marti: You always think that some big thing is going to happen and then you will know that you made it. And for me, at least, I still feel like I am just hanging on. It's like, when am I going to know that I made it? I never have had that moment of "A Ha! I'm here."

Matt: When would you recommend an artist first hire a manger?

Marti: For me, it was something that was good out of the gate. I didn't have any relationships or know anyone in the industry. If I was doing it again, I would say get a manager immediately.

Matt: How important is fan interaction to sustaining a career?

Marti: Critical. Unless there are fans of your music, no one cares. That was something that we always did. It is hard for me to do it now. But I run our websites. I am the one who responds to people. That means something to people if they are reaching out to you because your song affected them.

Matt: How important do you think geography is for a career in music?

Marti: Obviously, it is not critical. I did it without moving. But, it is certainly not the speedy route. It is easier to make connections and contacts when you live in a city that is music based. It is not critical, but it is helpful.

Matt: What general advice would you give to a new artist?

Marti: The hardest thing to take is constant rejection and constant criticism. You really have to believe in yourself. If you don't, you will never make it. And you have to be tough. We shopped Girl Next Door to Universal five times. And five times they said "No, we don't think this is anything." Then, it went on the radio and they said, "About that record." So, you have to believe in your music and in what you are doing and remember that everybody has been turned down. Madonna got turned down. Aerosmith got turned down. Somebody thought they were nobody at some point.

Derek Webb

Matt: Did you have any bands or attempts at pursuing a career in music before Caedmon's Call?

Derek: Yeah, kind of. I played in various bands all through high school. A ton of really bad rock and roll cover bands. It was the Eighties, so a lot of it is forgivable. I played in a ton of bands.

I was introduced to Cliff Young by Aaron Tate, who was then Caedmon's songwriter. He and I ended up splitting that work up over the years. Aaron and I went to high school together. Aaron and Cliff went to high school together. So Aaron was thing that connected us.

Typically, early on I was in a support role. I was a guitar player. I wasn't a singer or a songwriter. Those are the only two things in my job description now. I was just a guitar player. I didn't do anything else. I wrote a bunch of bad songs in high school. But, who didn't? When I first got into Caedmon's it was just to be a guitar player. Aaron didn't want to play in the band. He was just writing songs for the band. Cliff couldn't play guitar that well. So, they needed someone to play the guitar and it was just me. Just having a community of people and some outlet for creativity, I wound up writing some songs and eventually singing more, and ended up in the role that I did.

Matt: When you first began to play with Caedman's, what was the goal of the band? Were you playing for fun or to have a career?

Derek: I don't really know. That's a good question. I'm trying to think about it. I think we probably just saw a unique set of circumstances in front of us. We thought we had great songs because Aaron Tate is such a genius songwriter. That was the biggest compulsion for me, this amazing material. We were chasing down the opportunities at the time. Everyone was starting college. I didn't really go to college. Some of the other guys were splashing their feet in college a little bit. Cliff's dad is a big pastor in Texas and they had a full-fledged recording studio in their church and there was a possibility that we could go record some music. There was just this series of opportunities that we chased after.

All the best work the band did was chasing opportunities. Then a friend got us a gig at Rice University. Then, we had a little thing that we pressed onto some cassettes with a few more songs. Then, some other friends got us some gigs at some other colleges in Texas. We started making drives on the weekend.

Literally, it was like that. And I think when the band got into seasons of doing not as good of creative work was when we stopped chasing opportunities and started trying to create opportunities. That's really what it was. I don't think we had a plan.

Matt: Can you tell me about the details of the band getting signed to Warner Alliance?

Derek: We were actually in the process of working on a second indie record that we only got about five or six songs into before this opportunity came up. We were really resistant to doing anything that connected us in any way to the city of Nashville. At the time that seemed like the enemy.

We were Christians, but we didn't want that to have anything to do necessarily with the music that we were making. That just happens to be the way that we look at the world. Every artist has a way they look at the world, some grid that they look at the world to help them make sense of what they are seeing. Everybody has that. We wanted that to be true of us, like anybody else. We would take opportunities in proportion to the reality of our lives to write songs that had some spiritual content. But, on the whole, we weren't interested in that as much as just trying to write great songs.

We didn't want to go to Nashville because that is where all of the Christian music was coming from, the very narrowly categorized

'Christian music,' a lot of which we didn't like or respect. We didn't listen to it. It didn't have anything to do with what we were doing.

This guy, Wayne Watson, who was a real big Christian music star at the time, his son went to a college in Oklahoma. We had played a gig there. By the time were grooming to do this record deal, we were really making it work. We were touring in busses. We were going in to debt, but we were touring in busses. We were playing shows for hundreds of people, thousands in some parts of the country. We played in Oklahoma at this school. His son had gotten our indie record and passed it on to his dad. He asked if he had heard of us.

Wayne, having a production deal with Warner Alliance, took an interest, and also heard that Cliff's dad was this pastor in town that he knew. Wayne called Cliff's dad because he knew him. The next thing you know, we were sitting in Cliff's house in Houston. Wayne didn't live in Nashville. He lived in Houston, which we thought was kind of cool. We sat down with him. We explained our reluctancy to want to get involved with that sort of thing and he understood. He explained that he was with Warner Alliance and it was a unique situation because it is different from what you are used to in terms of a Christian label. They are actually part of Warner Brothers, but they are an imprint that does more Christian stuff. We told Wayne that we were not going to Nashville. So, Wayne brought guys from Nashville to Houston. Warner Alliance did not want to change what Caedmon's was doing. They just wanted to allow us to do it on a grander scale. We eventually wound up signing a deal with them and putting out a few records.

Matt: What did Caedmon's do to build up your fan base for tours?

Derek: Man, there was no Internet. People can't imagine a world with no Internet now. But, Al Gore hadn't turned it on yet. Looking back, I don't see how we did it or why. It was really hard. The first bit of marketing, if you want to call it that, was word of mouth. We were college-aged, a lot of people who were our age were able to get us gigs. Eventually, we figured out that we are not distributed anywhere and there is no way for anyone to have heard our stuff or know our stuff. It is hard to make a seven hour drive to play for fifteen people. You'd have to make four or five trips to that college before you could get a hundred people.

So, we made cassettes, which were readily copyable. We put a handful of tunes on it with a little bit of interviews in between with us talking about the tunes. It was like a little sampler. We put them in these little cassette sleeves. Whenever we had a gig at the colleges, we would send a box of these to whoever was promoting the gig and tell them to give them away and tell the people they gave them to to make copies for everybody else. It didn't cost us very much to make these cassettes.

Matt: Was that your idea? It sounds like the beginning of Noise Trade.

Derek: Right! Giving away free music, man. So, that's what we did initially. When we got there, people had something to attach to us in terms of our personalities and our music.

Beyond that, on all of our indie records, we would take the place where it says 'It is unlawful to copy' and change the language where it looked like the same statement to say 'Please make as many copies of this as possible and give it to everybody. Please help our music be heard.' All we wanted was people in front of us. People to play for. Places to go work.

Matt: You were one of the founding members of the Square Peg Alliance, and we have seen what Ten Out of Tenn is doing. What do you think the benefits are of cross-promotion among artists and some tangible benefits that you have seen from that?

Derek: It is hard to say. With all of the clatter of all these hundred million MySpace bands, there is just so much music out there now that people have to wade through to find anything that they like. I think it is really helpful when artists that you like lock arms with artists who make music that they like. That is an easy way for the artist's fans to find their way to people that they would very likely be into. That was our initial thought with Square Peg.

At the time, we didn't have a word for it, but what wound up being coined by Chris Anderson is "The Long Tail." The aggregate of 100,000 artists, none of whom have more than 1000 fans, amounts to more fans than the two percent of artists who are selling the majority of the records. You've got this really tall, really narrow head of the tail, and there will always be that. You will always have a pop market. There will always be a market for hits. There are fewer people having them now than ever before. And those people are selling fewer than ever before, but there is still that tall narrow head.

Then, immediately, it drops dramatically and the tail of this curve goes out as far as the eye can see, and me and and my wife, and all of the people in Ten Out of Tenn are in the tail somewhere. Some of us are closer to the head, some of us are closer to the tail.

Matt: Do you think that for an artist to be able to capitalize on Noise Trade, where you are giving away music for free in exchange for exposure, that the artist has to be touring?

Derek: I don't think as a rule. My wife doesn't tour a lot and has been out of a season of touring for awhile. She does really really well. Noise

Trade has been a tremendous benefit for her. She has done a lot of downloads. She makes great money every month. She continues to build her fan base. She has more than 20,000 people on her email list now.

Having the affection of 20,000 people who you also have information for is something you can monetize without touring. She is about to come out with a live record. Being able to tell 20,000 people, many of whom have never given you a penny, but have a lot of affection for you because you have given them something, which has caused them a great deal of shame because of the RIAA and a lot of other people, based on laws that will change in the very near future, that is a great thing. That is a lot of affection for her brand, so to speak. There is a big difference between promoting to 2,000 and to 20,000. Her career is self-sustaining just on her email list and barely doing any shows.

If you are going to get out and tour, you can do it on another level. At that point you are able to filter by zip code and tour more smartly. You can figure out what cities are better cities for you. Where do you have bigger markets? You can take a risk on a room that otherwise might be a bigger risk.

It happened to me when I first gave away *Mockingbird* before Radiohead and Trent [Reznor] and Prince and everybody else. We thought it was crazy at the time. But the moment where the light bulb started to go off for us is when we were sitting on 85,000 email addresses and zip codes of these people who had all downloaded my record. We looked at the top cities and New York and L.A. were in the top five. I had never toured in a solo artist in either city. What business does a little folk singer being down in the niche where I am have going to L.A. or New York. I never would have thought. But the numbers speak for themselves.

So, we booked a show in L.A. on a Wednesday night at a room on Hollywood that held 100 people at some little club with a zero guarantee, but ninety percent of the door. We thought, let's take a chance. Let's see if this thing works. We had 3,000 people within twenty miles of the venue that had downloaded the record.

The show sold out in two seconds. We turned fifty or sixty people away. They booked me into the bigger room that same night. I came back four months later and sold that one out. And eventually ended up selling their biggest room out at four hundred people. Now, I'm looking for a bigger room in L.A. I never would have known about that market if it wasn't for letting my record pass from friend to friend, with information for every person coming back to me.

That's why, in the long run, I probably made money giving my record away, as opposed to losing money. The opportunity cost is almost zero when you know how to use the information to your advantage and you can monetize further down the road. You can use the information to build a fan base on which you can have a career for twenty years. Having a direct meaningful connection to fans is a long-term career benefit. So, touring takes it to another level, but it is not required to make money.

Matt: How important is geography and location when you are starting a career in music?

Derek: I think when you are first starting out, it is better to be a big fish in a small pond. I recommend against anyone moving to Nashville to get into music – out of one side of my mouth. Everybody in town, from the guy who delivers my mail to the person who makes my latte, has a publishing deal and is trying to write songs and break in. I didn't move to Nashville for music. I moved there chasing a girl. I love it. It's a great town. Its good to be close to the people you are in business with so that you can go to their office and agitate them. But, I don't recommend it.

But then, out of the other side of my mouth, I will say that the indie music community in Nashville is a really small community. Ten Out of Tenn is a great example of this. The people we wind up working with, and being friends with, and touring with, and having play on records with us, aren't some top-dollar musicians who are the best in town that everybody knows. They are our friends. They are people who we like to drink wine on our porch with.

When people say, how would I be a drummer to play on your record? I'm like, 'Come move into my neighborhood forever. Come and be my neighbor and be in our community.' I don't know how you do that. But, those are the people who are getting in. It's a very inbred little community – in a good way. We all have home studios. We just wind up working together. So, proximity is pretty major in that regard.

But those communities could exist in any city. If you are in a city with no musicians, and you are at liberty to be somewhere with other musicians, you should. Like any life-season, you need to be in a community of people for it to work or thrive. Don't try to do it by yourself. Get people around you who are doing it and working on it. Sit together and be together and encourage each other. That is what it is gonna take. It is gonna get really hard. I didn't realize that early on because I was in Caedmon's and we had each other.

Once you are at a different stage as an artist and you are starting to tour, there is a reason that Nashville is Nashville. Look how many major cities you can get to from Nashville. It's a great hub to tour from, all of the touring companies are based there because you can get to all of these places. You can play in Birmingham, Knoxville, Atlanta, everywhere from Nashville. Whatever region you think your music makes sense in, whether it is the Midwest or the Northeast, or the West Coast, there are places like Nashville. It is good to hub professionally out of a city that integrates well in to your lifestyle. From Nashville, I can drive to a lot of places. Costs come down. I can spend more time with my family.

But coming to Nashville to get discovered is like being a needle and jumping into a haystack. You are not gonna get discovered, unless something really crazy-special happens. But don't stake your career on something crazy and special happening. Don't go get on American Idol. Caedmon's made it because we were in Houston, Texas. There was no music scene there. We were a band in that city doing something that no one else was doing and it helped get us attention. If you are doing something great and in a self-sustaining way, you are not going to be able to avoid attention.

I would rather see somebody do that locally and have a home town, have a place to come home to and have fans there, that supports you and is a home base for you. Nashville is not a home base for anybody. That's the thing that sucks about being in Nashville. Its hard for anyone to play a show in Nashville, especially people who live there. You don't come back to Nashville and play your big finale show because it's Nashville. Everybody's got their arms folded with their heads cocked to the side because they are either a critic or are looking at you like you are competition.

Matt: You left a well-known group to go solo. Almost all new artists will not have a pre-existing fan base. What advice would you give for an up and coming artist to be able to make a career with their music today, if you could speak directly to them?

Derek: I would say, rather than chasing the dream of impacting millions, really focus on trying to impact five hundred people. Try to connect more deeply with fewer people. Give more of yourself to fewer people and focus on those people.

Take advantage of all of the things that the Internet affords. Don't manufacture unless you have to. Keep it digital. Spend as little money as you can. Approach it like you are starting a small business. That's really what you are doing. It's blue-collar work. It is not fame and fortune. And, if it is, it is not that. Ask the people who have it.

A career in music is a real job. You have to work really hard at it. It is like any small business, where you will have a few years where you won't make any profit. You have to be ready for that. Go into some debt if you have to. It is work that you will really enjoy as long as your expectations are set right.

Playing music is a real job and you can do it. It just requires that your expectations are gauged correctly.

Embrace the depths of whatever niche you are. Whatever it is, embrace it, rather than trying to homogenize and be something that is prepped for mass consumption. Embrace that you may have very few fans. But, if you can pour yourself into those fans enough, you won't need very many of them to have a career for a long time. You might not be famous and you may not have more than enough money to pay your rent and your gas to and from the cities. But, it is a job and you can do it.

I'd recommend getting into Seth Godin and reading *Tribes*. There is an essay online called 1000 True Fans that lays the economy out of why you really only need about a thousand people who are super-devoted to what you are doing and support you to make a living. As long as you can be satisfied with that, that is really all it takes. It is not impossible. It is not this big mystery that it used to be.

More specifically, pick five cities that are close-by and you feel like you could go play shows in. Make it your goal over the next year to get one hundred people. Find a room that is appropriate for the kind of music you play, be it a bar, a college or a church, or whatever it is. Develop a relationship with that particular venue. Work all year to get a hundred people in five cities. Once you can do that, work to get two hundred people in five cities.

After that, add five more cities and try to get one hundred in those cities. It doesn't take but a few years until you are up to about twenty or thirty cities. If you can get two hundred people in thirty cities, and go to all of those cities three times a year, just routing your way around, you will have a vibrant career. You will make plenty of money. Vou-lah! You have a career. You have a job.

What that means is making good connections, harvesting information, really working hard to know who those fans are and make impressions with them, and to not look over those people's heads for your future fans. Look all those people in the face. Confess to the fact that you all need each other. They need your art in their lives and you need them to sustain you. Don't go the other way of disappearing into the mystique of the limo when the show is over. Pour yourself into those people.

In Caedmon's, we used to tell people in every college town where we played, 'We are going to IHop after the show.' Everybody come. It would be Caedmon's Call, party of sixty five. We would bounce around from table to table. By our second year, we knew two-thirds of the people at every show. I still know a lot of those people. As I travel the country, I hang out with them. I call them on my way into town and have meals with them and their families as we have all gotten older.

That's what it is all about. It is relational. Don't kid yourself and say that it is not. It is blue collar work. You need those people as much as they need you. The more you can embrace that, the easier time you are going to have.

ABOUT THE AUTHORS

Matthew Crumpton, Esq.

Matt Crumpton is an attorney, songwriter, entrepreneur, and philanthropist. He is the founder of Music Loves Ohio, a non-profit organization that gives opportunities to underserved youth to learn, record, and perform music. In addition to practicing small business and entertainment law, he has released three solo records and plays bass and keys in a Nineties rap cover band called The Winnie Cooper Project. Prior to law school, he worked backstage as a production assistant for Live Nation, managed bands, and promoted concerts. He lives in Columbus, Ohio.

Tristan Kinsley

Tristan Kinsley is a musician, songwriter, producer, engineer, and entrepreneur. He was a singer/guitarist in the folk-rock band, The Princes of Hollywood, where he learned much about the "real" music business. He plays guitar, pedal steel, dobro, lap steel, mandolin, banjo, and bass. While he continues to write and perform with a number of musicians, he spends much of his time as the owner and operator of The Wine Shoppe at Green Hills. He lives in Nashville, Tennessee with his wife Carrie.

THANK YOU

Thank you to: all of the artist interviewees for their time and candor in their talks with us; Kim Crumpton (for inspiring the idea for the book), Lee Bass, Zack Cramp, Ben Albaugh, Maria Schied (our wonderful editors), Claudia Lyster, Nettwerk, Mick Management, Matt Mangano, Carrie Kinsley, Bob Kinsley, Velvet Wildermuth, Mark Crumpton; Natalie Crumpton, and everyone who read this book.

For more information, please visit us online at http://www.makingitbook.com.

www.ingramcontent.com/pod-product-compliance
Lightning Source LLC
LaVergne TN
LVHW051511080426
835509LV00017B/2024

* 9 7 8 0 5 7 8 0 8 3 1 8 6 *